Even with Cracked Wings, I Choose You

Conversations on Love, Legacy, and Rebuilding

A book of love letters to Black men

By Della Owens

Dedication

Beloved, come close.

Before you turn this page, I want you to breathe, not that shallow kind we've been surviving on, but a breath from deep down... from where your grandmama's prayers still hum.

This ain't just paper and ink. No, baby. This is a homecoming. A slow unwrapping of all that heavy you were told you had to wear. It's a place where your armor can rest and your spirit can speak, finally. These are love notes carved in the dark— written with hands that trembled, but kept writing anyway. For you. For us. For what we almost forgot we could be to one another.

See, truth don't always holler. Sometimes it comes soft—like a whisper in the hush before dawn. But even soft truth leaves a mark. And this truth, Beloved? It's that I see you. Not the mask, not the myth. You.

This ain't no saving mission. Lord, no. You ain't broken. You're burdened. And I came to honor that weight, not pretend it ain't there. Even with wings chipped and stories scarred, you are still worthy of love that don't flinch.

Each chapter is a letter—written from the porch of my becoming, where the wind still carries the scent of memory and hope. These are not neat words. These are necessary ones. The kind that hold you when the world forgets how.

So come on. Sit with me a while. Let's remember who we were before the forgetting. Let's rebuild the we that still lives beneath the rubble.

With reverence and readiness,
—Always, Me

Foreword

Beloved,

There are words that you find when you need them most. Words that slip between the cracks of your armor and touch the places you've kept hidden even from yourself. Words that arrive not as judgment, but as recognition. Not as demand, but as offering. Not as criticism, but as the most profound kind of love.

This book was born from that intention to create a sanctuary of words for Black men who have carried so much, for so long, with so little acknowledgment of the weight.

When I began writing these letters, I didn't know exactly where they would lead. I only knew there was something that needed saying. Something about the particular journey of Black men in this world how you navigate spaces that weren't designed for your thriving, how you create dignity where others would strip it away, how you find ways to remain soft in a world that has given you every reason to harden.

I wanted to speak to that journey. Not from a distance, but from the intimate space of one heart recognizing another. Not with the clinical detachment of analysis, but with the tender attention of love that sees clearly and chooses anyway.

These letters don't pretend to capture every Black man's experience. How could they? The tapestry of Black masculine identity is too rich, too varied, too complex for any single narrative to contain. What these letters offer instead is a witnessing of the struggles rarely spoken, the tenderness often hidden, the dreams sometimes deferred but never fully abandoned.

They speak to the man who has been told his emotions make him weak, when in truth, they make him whole. They speak to the man who has been viewed as threat when all he offered was presence. They speak to the man who has been expected to provide without being nurtured, to protect without being protected, to remain strong without ever acknowledging pain.

But most of all, these letters speak to the man beneath those expectations the one who contains multitudes. The one who knows both strength and tenderness, both resilience and vulnerability, both the capacity to endure and the longing to be held.

That man deserves to be seen. To be honored. To be loved not for what he can do or provide or represent, but for who he is in his complete, complex humanity.

If you are that man, I hope these words find the tender places in you not to wound, but to heal. Not to expose, but to shelter. Not to demand more, but to say what has too rarely been said: I see you. I honor your journey. I recognize the weight you carry and the grace with which you carry it.

And if you love a Black man as father, son, brother, partner, friend I hope these letters help you see him more fully. Not just his strength, but his softness. Not just his resilience, but his need for rest. Not just what he offers to others, but what he himself deserves.

These pages hold no prescription for how Black men should be. No checklist of expectations to fulfill. No demands disguised as support.

Only recognition.

Only witnessing.

Only love that doesn't require perfection to persist.

Because even with cracked wings, perhaps especially with cracked wings, you are worthy of being chosen.

Of being seen.

Of being loved not in spite of your humanity, but because of it.

May these words find you when you need them most. May they remind you of what you've perhaps always known but the world has tried to make you forget: that your full humanity with all its strength and softness, all its power and vulnerability, all its certainty and questioning is not just acceptable, but essential. Not just tolerable, but beautiful. Not just enough, but exactly what this world needs.

With love that recognizes, chooses, and remains,

Della Owens

Contents

Chapter 1: The Weight You Were Never Meant to Carry.....................1

Chapter 2: You Weren't Made to Walk This Alone................................7

Chapter 3: When We Forgot We Were on the Same Side 13

Chapter 4: Your Pain Was Always Talking - Even in the Quiet..........20

Chapter 5: What If Soft Was Always Strong?.....................................26

Chapter 6: You Loved Us the Only Way You Knew How...................33

Chapter 7: Let's Rebuild Without Bleeding on Each Other 40

Chapter 8: I Still Believe in Black Love's Becoming..........................47

Chapter 9: Love Me Past the Masks and Muscle 54

Chapter 10: Beloved, You Were Never My Enemy..............................60

Chapter 11: Let's Grow Old in Joy, Not Just Survival.......................67

Chapter 12: Even with Cracked Wings, I Chose You 73

Chapter 13: The Dreams You Set Aside...80

Chapter 14: When the World Misreads Your Silence 86

Chapter 15: Your Body Carries Wisdom..92

Chapter 16: The Courage in Your Gentleness.....................................99

Chapter 17: Between Faith and Doubt 105

Chapter 18: The Legacy You're Already Building................................ 112

Chapter 19: When Laughter Becomes Your Shield and
            Your Medicine 118

Chapter 20: The Brotherhood You Need 124

Chapter 21: Reclaiming Your Narrative 131

Chapter 22: The Future Your Ancestors Dreamed 139

Chapter 1

The Weight You Were Never Meant to Carry

Dear Beloved,

I see you.

Not just the face you show to the world but the heaviness behind your eyes. That slow, quiet ache you've learned to dress in silence and strength. The kind of burden that don't make a sound but leaves bruises anyway. You've been carrying so much, for so long, that you've started to believe it's yours to carry.

But it's not. Not all of it.

Some of that weight? It was handed to you before you ever took your first breath. Passed down like a folded quilt, stitched with struggle, stitched with scarcity, stitched with someone else's pain. They said, "Be a man." But they never taught you how to be whole.

And so, you learned to wear the world like armor. To hold your tongue when you wanted to scream. To run headfirst into survival like it was the only path to respect.

But I need you to know something, right here at the start: That weight ain't all yours. It never was.

Your granddaddy carried some of it, too, when his hands were calloused from work that never paid what it owed. When he loved hard but didn't have the language for softness. When he showed up with his body but left parts of his spirit behind because the world didn't make room for both.

Your father, or the man who stood in his place, carried some of it too silently. Maybe with pride, maybe with pain, maybe with absence. Some of y'all lost him to death. Others to distance. And some of you never had him at all. Still, the weight found its way to you.

So now here you are. Tired. Maybe angry. Maybe numb.

And still, showing up.

Still laughing, even when the joy don't reach your chest. Still protecting, even when nobody noticed your wounds. Still loving, even when the love wasn't soft enough to hold you back.

I want to tell you today that your strength is not a question. But neither is your pain.

You are not weak for feeling weary. You are not broken for needing rest. And you damn sure aren't invisible; not to me.

I wrote this letter because I know what happens when Black men get used to being unseen. When you learn to make peace with pain like it's a roommate instead of a trespasser. When the world only applauds your endurance, not your existence.

I want to call you back, not to performance, but to presence. Not to proving, but to being.

Beloved, you don't have to hold it all. You never did.

There is room here to exhale. Room to grieve what no one ever helped you carry. Room to put the load down and let me sit beside it with you.

Because I didn't come to rescue you. I came to remember with you. To say aloud what should've been said long ago: I see the weight. I honor the cost. I still choose you.

I see how this world has asked too much of you, demanded your strength without offering sanctuary. How it's expected you to be both mountain and river, unmovable in your resolve yet fluid enough to navigate systems designed to break you. How it's praised your resilience while creating the very storms you've had to weather.

I see the nights you've lain awake, staring at ceilings that hold the weight of your unspoken worries. The mornings you've risen before the sun, carrying responsibilities that would crush lesser souls. The way you've learned to smile through pain so deep it's become part of your marrow.

This ain't just about the physical labor, though Lord knows your body has known work. It's about the emotional toll. The constant vigilance. The way you've had to calculate every word, every step, every breath in spaces that weren't built with your freedom in mind.

It's about how you've had to be ten steps ahead just to stay even. How you've had to swallow rage that had every right to be voiced. How you've had to prove your humanity in a world that too often questions it.

And through it all, you've remained. Standing. Breathing. Loving. Creating beauty from ashes and hope from heartache.

But Beloved, I need you to hear me: The weight of the world was never yours alone to carry. The burden of history was never yours alone to bear. The pain of generations was never yours alone to heal.

You were meant for more than just survival. You were meant for joy that reaches bone deep. You were meant for rest that restores, not just recharges. You were meant for love that sees all of you, not just what you can provide or protect.

I know what they told you. That Black men don't cry. That vulnerability is weakness. That your worth is tied to what you can endure, what you can produce, what you can prove.

But those are lies dressed in legacy's clothing.

Your tears are sacred. Your vulnerability is courage. Your worth was established long before you ever lifted a finger or shouldered a burden.

I want you to imagine, just for a moment, what it would feel like to put some of it down. Not all at once, I know that's too much to ask. But piece by piece. The expectations that were never fair. The standards that were always shifting. The masks that have grown heavy with wear.

What would it feel like to breathe without the weight? To laugh without the guard? To love without the fear?

I'm not promising it will be easy. Generations of conditioning don't dissolve overnight. But I am promising that I'll be here not to fix or to save, but to witness. To hold space. To remind you, again and again, that you are more than what you carry.

Because beneath the weight, there is still you. Brilliant, beautiful, boundless you. The you that dreams. The you that creates. The you that loves with a fierceness this world has rarely seen.

That's the you I see, even when the weight tries to obscure you. That's the you I choose, even when the burden makes you doubt your worth. That's the you I love, not in spite of your scars, but alongside them.

So, let's start here, with no fixing, no pretending. Just truth. Just you. Cracked wings and all.

With open arms and eyes that don't look away.

Always, Me

Chapter 2

You Weren't Made to Walk This Alone

Dear Beloved,

You've been holding it down so long, it's started to feel like a birthright. Like strength means standing alone. Like pride means silence. Like asking for help is a language you never got the dictionary for.

But let me remind you, because the world won't you weren't made to walk this road alone.

Somewhere along the way, you were taught that your worth was tied to how well you could suffer in silence. That manhood meant never needing. That to lean was to fail. But, Beloved, those are lies dressed up as legacy. Inherited myths passed down from wounded men who didn't have space to cry, or safe arms to fall into when it all felt like too much.

I ain't here to blame them. They were doing what they knew. But I am here to break it.

Because the truth is strength was never supposed to be lonely. And you were never meant to be the only pillar holding up the whole house.

You've been taught to be the answer. But who answers you?

You've been the safe space for so many. But where is your sanctuary?

Who checks on you when the lights go out and your chest gets tight from carrying too much too quietly?

This world has a way of celebrating your resilience while starving your humanity. They'll praise you for what you provide and overlook what you need. They'll say, "Be a man" and never explain that being a man doesn't mean being a fortress with no doors.

So, let's reframe this. Let's remember the truth.

You weren't born in isolation. You were born into community, wrapped in hands that held you before you could even speak your name. Before you could walk, somebody rocked you. Before you could feed yourself, someone offered you nourishment. You came into this world connected.

And you are still worthy of that connection.

There is no trophy for going it alone. No crown for pretending you don't need anyone. No prize for piling it on until your spirit breaks from the weight.

Let me ask you something nobody asks enough: Who's your safe place?

Who gets to see you when the titles fall away? When your voice cracks mid-sentence? When you don't have the right words, just a heavy pause and tired eyes?

I want to remind you; there is no shame in needing. No weakness in leaning.

Needing someone to hold you doesn't make you any less of a man. It makes you human. It makes you whole.

You deserve a love that sees past the performance. You deserve a hand to hold when the ground beneath you feels unsteady. You deserve to be reminded that you ain't out here by yourself even when it feels like it.

Beloved, I don't know what story taught you that love had to be earned through suffering. But I want to give you permission to unlearn it. You are allowed to be held. Allowed to be vulnerable. Allowed to say, "I can't do this by myself."

We come from people who knew how to gather. Who built homes from scraps and made soul food from scraps of soul. They may not have had much, but they had each other.

That's the inheritance I want you to claim.

Let me be clear: This is not a call to dependency. It's a call to interdependency, the sacred dance of leaning and lifting, giving and receiving, seeing and being seen.

I don't want you to shrink to fit someone's idea of strength. I want you to expand into the truth of who you are: A man who is allowed to rest. A man who is allowed to ask for help. A man who is allowed to be more than just what he carries.

I've watched you, Beloved. Watched how you've learned to walk with wounds that would have dropped lesser men to their knees. How you've carried burdens in silence because no one ever showed you where to set them down. How you've become so accustomed to standing alone that companionship almost feels like trespassing.

But that solitude? It was never the design. It was the detour.

Think about our ancestors; how they survived not through isolation but through connection. How they formed circles of protection, circles of prayer, circles of resistance. How they understood that to be separated was to be vulnerable, but to be together was to be fortified.

They knew something we've forgotten: that there is divine wisdom in community. That we were never meant to weather the storms alone, but to huddle close, to share warmth, to remind each other that dawn always follows the darkest night.

I see how hard it is for you to ask. How the words catch in your throat like fish bones. How you'd rather bleed quietly than admit you're wounded. How you've convinced yourself that needing is weakness, when in truth, it's the most human thing about you.

But what if I told you that your vulnerability is actually your superpower? That when you finally say, "I'm tired," or "I'm scared," or "I need you," you're not diminishing your strength, you're expanding it. You're creating space for a different kind of power. The kind that doesn't require you to stand alone, but invites others to stand with you.

There's a reason why the strongest trees have the deepest roots, intertwined underground with others in the forest. They understand that true resilience comes not from isolation, but from connection.

You don't have to be the exception to this natural law.

I know the world has taught you otherwise. I know how Black men have been conditioned to believe that independence is the only path to respect. How you've been shown, again and again, that to need is to be needy, to feel is to be weak, to ask is to be less than.

But Beloved, those lessons were never about protecting you. They were about controlling you. About keeping you from the very thing that might save you: community. Connection. The sacred knowledge that you are not, and have never been, alone in this struggle.

I've seen what happens when Black men try to carry it all. How the weight bends the spine. How the isolation breeds a particular kind of loneliness that no amount of achievement can fill. How the silence eventually becomes a prison, not a protection.

And I refuse to watch you disappear into that silence.

I refuse to let you believe that your strength must come at the cost of your softness.

I refuse to accept that your manhood must be measured by how much you can endure without breaking.

Because here's what I know for sure: the most powerful men I've ever known were not the ones who never needed, but the ones who knew how to ask. Who understood that vulnerability wasn't the opposite of strength, but its companion. Who recognized that true power lies not in how much you can carry alone, but in knowing when and how to share the load.

So, if no one's ever told you: I'm here. I see you. You don't have to do this alone. You never should have had to.

Let's walk together from here.

Cracked wings don't mean you can't fly. They just mean you'll need someone to catch the wind with you.

With love that does not flinch and presence that does not waver.

Always, Me

Chapter 3

When We Forgot We Were on the Same Side

Dear Beloved,

We didn't get here overnight.

This ache between us; the tension, the mistrust, the silence; it didn't just fall from the sky. It was built, brick by brick, over generations. Some of it was passed down in stories. Some in scars. Some in the things we never learned to say out loud.

We didn't forget each other by accident. We were taught to. Conditioned to. Divided long before we knew what unity ever looked like.

You and I, we were once each other's first home. Black men and Black women, rising from the same soil, carrying the same soul-memory of struggle and brilliance. We were the shelter and the song. We were survival and sweetness in the same breath. And then… the fractures came.

Not all at once. But slow.

Policies that pulled fathers from their homes. Welfare systems that rewarded distance. Media that painted you as threat, and me as bitter. Churches that preached your dominance and my submission but never taught us how to partner.

And the ache grew.

We started measuring who had it harder instead of holding space for each other's hurt. We got so used to surviving, we forgot how to soften. We confused protection with control. We replaced unity with quiet competition.

And before we knew it, we were looking at each other like strangers instead of soul kin.

But Beloved, let me say this as plain as I can: You are not my enemy. You never were.

I know the wounds run deep. I know the betrayal, the abandonment, the unmet expectations on both sides. I know the way some of our men left. I know the way some of our women hardened. I know the generational patterns that shaped our parents and bent our babies.

But I also know this: There's still a we in us. Buried under the rubble. Bruised by the struggle. But alive. Still breathing.

Somewhere between the "you always" and "you never," Between the silence and the shouting, Between the missed calls and the misread intentions. We forgot how to reach for each other.

But we can remember. We must.

This isn't about blame, it's about truth. It's about the mother who had to raise a son without the tools. It's about the father who couldn't teach what he was never taught. It's about the daughters who became caretakers before they could bloom. It's about the sons who became men in the shadows of absence.

And it's about us, standing in the middle of that legacy, choosing to break the pattern.

What if we stopped asking who hurt first and started asking what healing requires of both of us?

What if we laid down the scoreboard and picked up a mirror?

What if instead of defending our pain, we defended each other?

Beloved, I miss us.

I miss the way we used to protect each other with our presence. The way your laughter used to live in my chest. The way my love used to cover your name. I miss the quiet knowing that no matter what the world said, we were each other's people. Not perfect. But ours.

And maybe we can't go back. But we can go forward with truth.

Let's name the hurt.

Let's hold the grief.

Let's peel back the layers and see what's still living underneath.

Because despite the damage, there's still something holy here. Still, something worth rebuilding.

You are *not* my competition. You are *not* my project. You are *not* the wound. I refuse to confuse you with the ways this world tried to tear us apart.

You are my mirror.

My kin.

My possibility.

I think about how we got here sometimes. How the system set traps we didn't even see coming. How they knew that if they could separate us; Black men from Black women; they could weaken the whole cloth of our community. How they used economic pressure, mass incarceration, and cultural propaganda to convince us we were opponents instead of partners.

And it worked. For too long, it worked.

We started believing the lies they told about you; that you were dangerous, lazy, uncommitted. And you started believing the lies they told about us; that we were angry, demanding, impossible to please. We internalized narratives that were never ours to begin with, and we used them as weapons against each other.

I remember hearing stories about how it used to be. How Black love was resistance. How Black partnership was a revolution. How our ancestors understood that to survive the unimaginable, they needed each other not perfect, but present. Not flawless, but faithful.

They knew something we forgot: that our liberation is bound together. That when you rise, I rise. That your joy is my joy. That your pain, when I hold it with care, becomes lighter for both of us.

But somewhere along the way, we started competing for scraps instead of building tables together. We started keeping score; who had it worse, who sacrificed more, who stayed longer, who left first. We became so focused on our individual survival that we forgot our collective power.

I see it in the way we talk past each other now. In the way we've learned to expect disappointment. In the way we enter relationships already armored, already guarded, already preparing for what might go wrong instead of creating space for what could go right.

But Beloved, that's not who we are. That's not our truth. That's not the legacy our ancestors fought and died for.

Our truth is deeper than the division.

Our connection is older than the wounds.

Our love is stronger than the systems that tried to break it.

I know it's not simple. I know there's real hurt here; not imagined, not exaggerated. I know there are conversations we need to have that will feel like fire in our throats. I know there are apologies that need to be spoken and received. I know there is grief that needs to be honored before joy can fully return.

But I also know this: we are worth the work.

Worth the uncomfortable conversations.

Worth the vulnerable truths.

Worth the patient rebuilding.

Because when Black men and Black women remember we're on the same side, mountains move. When we lock arms instead of pointing fingers, healing happens. When we choose to see each other, really see each other, beyond the stereotypes and the scars, we reclaim something sacred.

So, I'm asking you to remember with me.

Remember how we used to finish each other's sentences. Remember how we used to pray over each other's dream. Remember how we used to stand between each other and danger without hesitation.

That memory isn't just nostalgia; it's a map back to each other.

I'm not asking for perfection. I'm not even asking for forgiveness yet. I'm just asking for presence. For willingness. For one brave step toward each other instead of another step away.

Because the truth is, Beloved, I'm tired of the distance. Tired of the misunderstanding. Tired of watching us wound each other when the world has already left enough scars.

I want to rebuild something beautiful with you.

Something honest.

Something that honors both our individual journeys and our shared destiny.

Something that doesn't require either of us to shrink or silence ourselves to make room for the other.

So, if you're ready, I'll meet you there;where the remembering begins. Where we drop the armor. Where we relearn each other's rhythms. Where love is not performance but presence.

Let's find our way back, not to the past, but to the promise of what we still can be.

Together.

With a hand outstretched and a heart wide open.

Always, Me

Chapter 4

Your Pain Was Always Talking - Even in the Quiet

Dear Beloved,

I heard you long before you ever said a word.

You may not have known it, but your pain's been speaking this whole time. Not in the loud ways that get attention. Not in explosions or breakdowns. But in the pauses. In the distance. In the way you shrink without meaning to. In the way your smile doesn't always reach your eyes. In the way you sometimes disappear, even when you're still in the room.

That's pain, Beloved. That's grief without a funeral. That's sorrow with no script.

And I know you've been told to tough it out. To move on. To keep pushing. But there is a difference between moving forward and pushing through. One is rooted in healing. The other is just survival wearing Sunday clothes.

And Lord knows you've survived a lot.

The losses that weren't named. The disappointments you buried under responsibility. The rage you tucked inside your chest because nobody ever taught you where it could safely land. The moments you wanted to cry but didn't know where the tears would fall if you started.

Your pain has been patient. But it's been present. All this time.

In the way you hold your breath when someone gets too close. In the way you retreat instead of reach. In the way you laugh too loud at things that don't feel funny anymore.

I see it. And I don't flinch.

Because I know this kind of ache it's ancestral. You weren't the first to carry it. And sadly, you weren't given the tools to put it down.

Somewhere along the way, Black men were taught that pain had to be hidden. That tears were weakness. That softness was dangerous. And so, generation after generation, you learned to go quiet instead of go inward. You learned to bottle instead of breathe. You learned to ache in silence.

But Beloved, silence don't mean healing. It just means the wound has gone underground.

I don't say this to shame you. I say this to free you.

Because your pain is valid. Even if it's quiet. Even if it showed up as numbness instead of tears. Even if it took the shape of anger, of withdrawal, of fatigue, of over-functioning, of always being the one who holds it down.

You've been carrying all of this, and nobody ever stopped long enough to say, "I see what it's costing you."

Well, I'm stopping now.

You don't have to make a speech. You don't have to crack open all at once. You don't even have to know where to begin.

Just know this your pain matters. Not because it's dramatic. Not because it's loud. But because it's yours.

You have the right to feel. The right to unravel. The right to not be okay all the time.

You don't have to be the strong one every hour of every day. You're not here to be a machine. You're here to be whole. And wholeness includes grief. Includes confusion. Includes moments when you sit in the dark, not knowing how to name what hurts.

And you are not alone in that darkness. I am here. Not to fix, but to witness. Not to pull you out, but to sit beside you until you're ready to rise.

I've watched you, Beloved, in those quiet moments when you thought no one was looking. When the mask slips just a little. When your shoulders drop under the weight of everything you've been carrying. When your eyes go distant, traveling to places you never speak of out loud.

I've seen the way certain songs make you go still. The way certain memories catch in your throat. The way certain dates on the calendar make you retreat into yourself, like you're bracing for an impact only you can feel.

That's your pain talking. And it deserves to be heard.

Not dismissed with "shake it off" or "man up" or "it's all in the past." Not drowned in distractions or numbed with whatever temporary relief this world offers. Not pushed down until it turns into something harder, something sharper, something that cuts you from the inside.

Your pain is trying to tell you something important. Something about what you've endured. Something about what you need. Something about the healing that's still waiting to happen.

I know it's scary to listen. I know you've been taught that acknowledging pain is the same as surrendering to it. That if you give it voice, it might swallow you whole. That if you start crying, you might never stop.

But Beloved, that's not how healing works.

Pain doesn't grow stronger when we face it it grows stronger when we run from it. When we pretend it isn't there. When we build our lives around avoiding it instead of moving through it.

I've seen what happens when Black men aren't given permission to grieve. How that unprocessed pain shows up in their bodies as high blood pressure, as insomnia, as tension that never fully releases. How it shows up in their relationships as walls too high for anyone to climb, as anger that flares without warning, as distance that no amount of physical closeness can bridge.

I've seen how it gets passed down, too. Father to son. Uncle to nephew. Brother to brother. This unspoken inheritance of swallowed sorrow. This silent agreement that pain is private, that vulnerability is dangerous, that strength means suffering alone.

But what if there's another way?

What if your pain, when given space to breathe, could become your teacher instead of your tormentor? What if your wounds, when tended with care, could become wisdom instead of weakness? What if your grief, when honored with patience, could become a gateway to a deeper kind of joy?

I believe this is possible. Not because I'm naive about how deep the hurt goes, but because I've witnessed the transformation that happens when pain is finally acknowledged. When it's met with compassion instead of criticism. When it's held in community instead of carried in isolation.

I've seen men who thought they were broken beyond repair find pieces of themselves they thought were lost forever. I've seen tears that were decades in the making finally fall, making way for a lightness that no amount of pretending could ever create.

24

I've seen healing happen not in grand, dramatic moments, but in quiet acts of courage. In the willingness to say, "this hurts." In the decision to reach for connection instead of retreating into familiar numbness. In the brave vulnerability of asking for help when the load gets too heavy.

Because even pain, when it's honored, can lead to healing. Even silence, when held with love, can become a song. Even numbness, when met with gentleness, can soften into feeling again.

So, if today is heavy, let it be heavy. Let yourself be human.

You don't have to justify your ache. You don't have to defend your wounds. You just have to give them room to breathe.

And when you do, Beloved, you'll find that pain doesn't last forever, not when it's met with truth. Not when it's finally allowed to speak.

So speak, if you're ready. Or sit in the silence a little longer if you need to.

Either way, I'm still here. Loving you. Hearing you. Even in the quiet.

With deep listening and open arms,

Always, Me

Chapter 5

What If Soft Was Always Strong?

Dear Beloved,

What if we've had it wrong all along?

What if the strength you were taught to reach for the grit, the silence, the stoicism was only half the story?

What if strength didn't look like holding it all together... but knowing when to let yourself fall apart in peace?

What if strength wasn't how well you could hide the hurt, but how bravely you could feel it?

Beloved, I need you to sit with this: What if soft was always strong?

I know.

Softness has been painted as weakness for far too long. Especially for you for the Black man, expected to be stone, to never break, to never flinch.

The world told you that to be soft was to be vulnerable. And to be vulnerable was to be unsafe. And so you built up layers walls made of pride, silence, and self-denial.

But here's the truth no one said loud enough: Your softness is not a threat. It is a power.

The way your voice drops when you're comforting a child? Strength. The way your tears rise when you remember a loss? Strength. The way you want to be held without having to perform or produce anything? Strength. The way you crave tenderness but were told to bury it? Still strength.

You have been strong in ways the world didn't know how to honor.

But let's do something radical here. Let's rewrite the definition.

What if your softness is your sanctuary? What if it's where your truest self lives not behind the armor, but underneath it?

Beloved, I know what you were taught.

Be hard.

Be quiet.

Be unshakable.

But being unshakable doesn't mean being untouched. It doesn't mean losing your humanity to fit into someone else's idea of what a "real man" should be.

You were never meant to be granite. You were meant to be whole.

And wholeness includes softness. It includes the nights when you cry alone in the dark. The mornings when you need someone to tell you they're proud of you not for what you've done, but for who you are. The moments when you long for softness, but fear it might be used against you.

Let me say this gently and with conviction:

Softness is not surrender.

Softness is not shame.

Softness is not failure.

Softness is resistance in a world that told you love had to be earned through labor. Softness is rebellion against a narrative that stripped you of your right to feel. Softness is remembering that you are not just a provider, not just a protector, you are a person. A soul. A spirit. Deserving of tenderness.

There is nothing weak about needing affection. About longing to be understood. About asking for peace over pressure.

Softness says: "I'm not afraid to be seen in all my forms." And that's the kind of strength this world needs more of.

I've watched you, Beloved, in those rare moments when you let your guard down. When you think no one's looking. When the weight of always being "the strong one" gets too heavy to bear. I've seen how your shoulders drop, how your breath changes, how something in your eyes shifts from vigilance to vulnerability.

And in those moments, you've never looked more powerful to me.

Because it takes courage to be soft in a world that told you hardness was the only way to survive. It takes bravery to feel in a culture that taught you numbness was safer. It takes strength to show tenderness when everything around you said tenderness made you a target.

I think about our ancestors, how they survived unspeakable hardship not by becoming stone, but by preserving their humanity against all odds. How they sang songs of sorrow and joy. How they created art and music that still moves us generations later. How they loved fiercely, laughed deeply, and held each other through the darkest nights.

That wasn't weakness. That was revolutionary resistance.

They understood something we've forgotten: that softness is not the absence of strength, but its most profound expression.

Look at the oak tree that bends in the storm while the rigid pine snaps. Look at water that can carve through mountains not through force, but through persistence and flexibility. Look at how the strongest metals must be tempered, heated, cooled, and made malleable before they reach their full potential.

Nature knows what we've denied: true strength requires softness.

I know this isn't easy to hear, much less to embody. The world has given you so many reasons to armor up. To believe that your safety lies in impenetrability. To equate emotion with weakness and stoicism with power.

Every movie hero who never flinched. Every father who told you to "man up." Every playground taunt of "soft" thrown like it was the worst thing a boy could be. Every time vulnerability was met with rejection or ridicule.

These experiences taught you to build walls, not bridges. To swallow tears instead of letting them flow. To clench your jaw instead of opening your heart.

And I understand why. Those walls protected you. That silence preserved you. That hardness helped you navigate spaces that weren't safe for your softness.

But Beloved, what protected you then may be limiting you now.

Those walls that kept pain out also keep love at a distance. That silence that prevented ridicule also prevents connection. That hardness that earned respect also creates loneliness.

What if there's another way to be strong? A way that doesn't require you to sacrifice parts of yourself? A way that allows you to be both powerful and tender, both resilient and receptive, both steadfast and soft?

I believe there is. I've glimpsed it in you in the way you sometimes let yourself be held. In the way your eyes well up during certain songs. In the way you touch things gently when you think no one's watching. In the way you love, when you feel safe enough to let that love fully express itself.

That's not your weakness showing. That's your wholeness emerging.

So go ahead. Be the man who says I'm tired. Be the man who says I love you and means it in more than physical touch. Be the man who hugs his son tight and tells him it's okay to cry. Be the man who holds his daughter close and shows her that tenderness isn't a woman's trait it's a human one. Be the man who isn't afraid to bloom.

You don't have to trade your power for peace. You don't have to sacrifice your softness to be safe. You don't have to be hard to be worthy. You already are.

I see the strength in your softness. The courage it takes to open up when you've been told to shut it all down. The bravery it takes to love without guarantees. The fire it takes to let your heart remain breakable in a world that tried to harden you.

That, Beloved, is the kind of strong that lasts.

So, what if just for today you let your softness lead? Let it speak. Let it stretch. Let it show you a new kind of freedom.

And when the world tries to tell you otherwise, just smile and say: "I know what real strength looks like. I see it in my softness."

With tenderness that honors every layer of you.

Always, Me

Chapter 6

You Loved Us the Only Way You Knew How

Dear Beloved,

Let me start here: thank you.

Not for perfection. Not for always getting it right. But for the trying. For the showing up, even when you didn't know how. For the ways you loved us that didn't always look like love but were rooted in it just the same.

See, there's a version of you one the world never got to know who loved with his whole chest but didn't have the words for it. A version that gave what he had, not because it was all he wanted to give, but because it was all he had been taught.

And I want to say this with my whole soul: That version of you deserves to be seen, too.

I know you carried so much. The pressure to protect without the blueprint. The demand to provide without complaint. The responsibility to be everything for everyone even when you were running on empty.

And still, you gave.

Maybe you didn't say "I love you" in words, but we heard it in the way you worked long hours with tired hands. Maybe you didn't always know how to be emotionally present, but you made sure there was food on the table and a roof overhead. Maybe you didn't know how to talk about feelings, but we saw you pacing the floor when we were sick, holding your breath when we were out too long, trying to hold the world back with your bare hands.

That's love. It may not be the kind the movies show, but it's the kind we lived. It's the kind that matters.

You see, so many of our fathers, brothers, uncles, and sons were taught that love had to be hard, had to come wrapped in sacrifice and stoicism. And so, they gave what they had: provision, protection, presence in the ways they understood.

But Beloved, what if I told you, it was enough? Not perfect, not painless but enough to deserve honor.

Because while some people had guidance, you had grit. While others had therapy, you had trial and error. While some were handed tools, you were handed trauma and still, you chose to love anyway.

And yes, there were times you got it wrong. Times when silence cut deeper than words ever could. Times when absence left a mark. Times when pride felt louder than apology.

But this isn't just about the harm. This is about the humanity underneath it.

You were trying to love us while carrying wounds no one gave you space to name. Trying to lead us when you were still learning how to walk unafraid. Trying to offer shelter while weathering storms that started long before you were born.

I think about the men who raised you, Beloved. How they too were doing the best they could with what little they had been given. How they passed down both their strengths and their scars. How they taught you to be a man in the only ways they knew how sometimes tender, sometimes tough, always trying to prepare you for a world they knew wouldn't be gentle with your Black body or your beautiful spirit.

I think about how love got tangled up with survival for our people. How providing became the primary language of care when words failed or felt too risky. How protection became paramount when the world offered so many threats. How presence just the sheer act of staying when so many forces tried to pull you away became its own kind of devotion.

And in that context, your love makes perfect sense.

You learned to love practically before you learned to love poetically. You learned to love through doing before you learned to love through saying. You learned to love protectively before you learned to love vulnerably.

And there is such beauty in that kind of love, even with its limitations.

I remember watching you, how your eyes would soften when you thought no one was looking. How your hands, so strong from labor, would become gentle when touching something precious. How your voice, often firm from having to command respect in a world that tried to diminish you, would drop to a whisper when speaking words of care.

Those moments revealed the tenderness that lived beneath the toughness. The softness that survived despite everything that tried to harden you. The love that found its way through cracks in the armor you were told you had to wear.

And that love, imperfect as it sometimes was, still nourished us.

Still shaped us.

Still mattered.

I know there were times when you wished you could give more. When you wanted to find the words but they stuck in your throat. When you longed to express the depth of your feeling but weren't sure if it was safe to be that exposed. When you tried to love in ways you'd never been shown and stumbled in the attempt.

Those moments weren't failures, Beloved. They were brave attempts at breaking cycles. They were silent revolutions against generational patterns. They were love trying to evolve, even without a roadmap.

And I saw them. I honored them then, and I honor them now.

Because loving while wounded is one of the most courageous acts I know. Giving while depleted is one of the most generous. Staying present while fighting your own demons is one of the most faithful.

You may have been raised by men who never hugged you, never told you they were proud. Men who taught you toughness but not tenderness. Who confused control with care and silence with strength.

But you, you loved us anyway.

And I don't want to let that go unnoticed. I don't want the effort to disappear in the shadow of imperfection.

You did the best you could with what you had. And some days, that had to be enough. Some days, it was everything.

I think about the legacy you're creating now. How your love, even with its rough edges, is still teaching. How your willingness to try, to grow, to reach beyond what was modeled for you is creating new possibilities for those who come after you.

How every time you choose vulnerability over silence, you're showing another generation of Black men that there are multiple ways to be strong.

How every time you express affection without expectation, you're expanding the definition of masculinity for sons watching from the sidelines.

How every time you admit when you're wrong or when you're hurting, you're giving permission for others to do the same.

That's not just love, that's legacy. That's not just care, that's transformation.

And it matters, Beloved. It matters so much.

Because while we can acknowledge the ways love sometimes fell short, we must also celebrate the ways it showed up at all, especially against such tremendous odds.

In a world that has tried to separate Black men from their tenderness, your attempts to love however imperfect are acts of resistance.

In a society that has criminalized, dehumanized, and disposable ized Black men, your commitment to care however complicated is revolutionary.

In a culture that rarely acknowledges the emotional lives of Black men, your willingness to feel however quietly is radical.

So today, let me give you what maybe no one has: Grace. For the ways you tried. For the ways you grew. For the ways you protected even when you were tired of fighting.

And if no one has ever said it before, let me say it now, clearly and without hesitation: I see your effort. I see your heart beneath the hardness. I see the boy who wanted to be loved and the man who tried to love in return.

You loved us the only way you knew how. And that love flawed, fumbling, fierce still found its way to us.

Still shaped us.

Still matters.

So, here's to you, Beloved. For showing up when you didn't know how. For choosing presence even when you wanted to run. For giving what you had, even when it didn't look like much.

It was more than enough to be remembered. And from here forward, we don't have to keep loving in survival mode. We get to choose new ways. We get to love in wholeness. We get to rewrite the ending.

But before we build new, let me pause and honor what was:

The trying. The protecting. The effort born from a heart that didn't know how to say, "I love you," but never stopped meaning it.

With reverence for every flawed but faithful act of love.

Always, Me

Chapter 7

Let's Rebuild Without Bleeding on Each Other

Dear Beloved,

We've all been cut by something.

Words that stung and stayed. Hands that should've held but harmed instead. Silence where there should've been softness. Absence when what we needed was to be seen.

You know that kind of pain, the kind that doesn't just bruise the body, but bruises the spirit.

And if we're honest, we've both carried wounds so long they've turned into habits. Ways of protecting ourselves that started as survival but became walls we forgot how to lower.

This letter? It's not about pointing fingers. It's about opening palms.

Because we've hurt each other, sometimes without meaning to. Sometimes while trying to love. Sometimes while still learning how to love ourselves.

But we can't keep calling this normal. We can't keep passing down our pain like heirlooms and then wondering why our relationships feel more like battlegrounds than sanctuaries. We can't keep reenacting the same cycles expecting different outcomes, hoping love will grow in soil we haven't cleared of the weeds.

Beloved let's be the ones who stop the bleeding.

Let's be the ones who look at the wreckage, not with shame, but with intention. Let's stop wounding each other in the name of truth, when what we really need is tenderness. Let's stop reenacting our childhood scars on the people who didn't create them. Let's stop confusing boundaries with punishment, and silence with peace.

Because here's what I know for sure: Pain that isn't healed gets passed on. And love that isn't nurtured turns sharp.

I've seen it happen. You have too.

The daughter who becomes distant because no one taught her how to stay open. The son who turns cold because warmth made him feel exposed. The partner who pulls away not out of disinterest, but out of fear that if they lean in, they'll be left again.

We are carrying things our grandparents never had the space to speak. And we are acting them out in the kitchen, in the bedroom, in the quiet moments when our triggers talk louder than our intentions.

I've watched it in my own life how the wounds I never tended became weapons I never meant to wield. How the pain I tried to bury resurfaced in my reactions, my defenses, my inability to trust even when trust was earned. How the hurt places in me recognized and sometimes even created hurt places in others.

And I've seen it in you too, Beloved. The way certain words make you retreat into silence. The way certain tones make your shoulders tense, your jaw clench, your eyes go distant. The way you sometimes respond to present love with past fear, meeting tenderness with suspicion because tenderness hasn't always been safe.

This isn't your fault. Or mine.

We didn't choose the wounds that shaped us. We didn't write the first chapters of our stories. We didn't select the lessons that taught us love was conditional, that vulnerability was dangerous, that showing our full selves might lead to rejection or ridicule.

Those narratives were handed to us by family who did the best they could with their own unhealed places, by a society that profits from our disconnection, by systems that were never designed for our wholeness.

But what if we stopped?

What if we took one brave step back not to escape, but to examine? What if we told the truth about our trauma not just to share it, but to interrupt it? What if we committed to rebuilding not just differently, but deliberately?

I'm thinking about the legacy of hurt in our community. How slavery separated families and forced people to suppress their emotions just to survive. How Jim Crow taught Black folks that showing certain feelings could be deadly. How poverty created conditions where love had to take a backseat to survival. How mass incarceration continues to tear apart bonds that were meant to last lifetimes.

These aren't just historical footnotes; they're living wounds that still shape how we love, how we fight, how we heal, how we harm.

But history doesn't have to be destiny.

We can acknowledge these patterns without being defined by them. We can honor the pain without letting it dictate our future. We can recognize the triggers without pulling them on each other.

Beloved, I'm not asking for perfection.

I'm asking for presence.

I'm asking for pause.

I'm asking for you to sit with what's bleeding before it spills onto the people trying to love you.

And I promise to do the same.

To notice when my tone gets sharp because I'm afraid of being hurt again. To recognize when I'm testing your love instead of receiving it. To pause when old pain rises up and threatens to speak through my mouth in ways I'll regret.

We are not obligated to repeat what broke us.

We can love each other with healed hands.

We can speak to each other with softened tongues.

We can hold space without holding score.

But we can't do that if we keep pretending the pain isn't there.

Let's acknowledge it. Let's name it. Let's walk with it until it loses its grip.

I think about the courage this takes to look at our wounds without flinching, to examine our patterns without shame, to take responsibility for our healing without blaming ourselves for needing it.

This is sacred work, Beloved. Not the kind that gets applause or recognition. Not the kind that happens overnight. But the kind that changes legacies. The kind that creates new possibilities not just for us, but for everyone who comes after us.

Because healing isn't pretty, but it's possible. And freedom? It's waiting in the spaces where we stop defending our wounds and start tending to them.

I've seen glimpses of what this could look like. Moments when we've managed to pause before reacting. Times when we've chosen vulnerability over vengeance. Conversations where we've spoken our truth without using it as a weapon.

Those moments give me hope. They remind me that while the past has shaped us, it doesn't have to define us. That while we carry wounds, we also carry wisdom. That while we've inherited pain, we've also inherited resilience.

You and I; we don't have to keep reenacting the same scenes.

We can rewrite the script.

We can choose language that doesn't cut.

We can create homes that don't echo with old ghosts.

Let's rebuild, Beloved. Not on broken bricks, but on solid soil.

Let's build with clarity; with compassion; with consent.

Let's build knowing that we are worthy not because we've never been wounded, but because we've decided those wounds won't rule us anymore.

You deserve a love that doesn't come with collateral damage. You deserve peace that doesn't require pretending. You deserve a relationship where survival isn't the goal; healing is.

So, if you're ready, I am too. Let's lay it all out. Let the dust settle. Let the grief breathe.

And then, with steady hands and honest eyes, let's build something that doesn't make us bleed to stay inside it.

With tenderness and a trowel in hand.

Always, Me

Chapter 8

I Still Believe in Black Love's Becoming

Dear Beloved,

I still believe.

Not because it's always been easy. Not because the stories haven't held ache and absence. Not because we've always gotten it right.

I still believe in Black love because somehow through the wounds, through the silence, through the systems that tried to strangle it we are still here, reaching for each other.

That, Beloved, is nothing short of holy.

I believe in Black love not the polished kind, not the picture-perfect kind, but the kind that's real.

The kind that still smells like Sunday dinner and sounds like late night porch conversations. The kind that bends but doesn't break. The kind that knows your soul's rhythm before your lips can form the words.

I believe in love that can sit in the wreckage and still choose to rebuild.

Because our love has always had to be revolutionary. It's had to fight to exist. It's had to bloom through concrete, rise through red lines, outlive welfare policies, incarceration, miseducation, and mass distortion. It's had to survive being called everything but sacred.

And still, it does.

Beloved, you've been taught that Black love is hard. But that's not the whole truth.

The truth is, it's strong. The truth is, it's tender. The truth is, it's layered and luminous, built from laughter, resilience, and a refusal to let this world tell us we're unworthy of softness.

I believe in your love even when you don't say it out loud. Even when it shows up in acts instead of words. Even when you don't yet know how to let it land without fear.

I see how you want to love freely but were raised on restraint. I see how you protect before you allow it. How you offer without asking for anything in return. How you've learned to love through survival but are yearning for a love that doesn't feel like work.

And I see myself in you tired sometimes, guarded often, but still choosing love. Still showing up. Still hoping that this time, we'll get it right. That this time, we'll be met where we stand, not asked to bend or shrink or perform.

I think about how our ancestors loved against impossible odds. How they created ceremonies in secret, whispered vows under stars, passed down rings made from spoons because gold was forbidden. How they found ways to honor their commitments even when those commitments weren't legally recognized. How they built family from fragments, community from chaos.

That legacy lives in us, Beloved. That determination to love despite everything that says we shouldn't, couldn't, wouldn't be able to sustain it.

I think about how revolutionary it is, even now, for Black men and women to love each other tenderly in a world that has tried to pit us against each other. How radical it is to choose partnership when the narratives around us often emphasize division. How brave it is to be vulnerable when vulnerability has historically made us targets.

And yet, here we are.

Still reaching.

Still trying.

Still believing.

Because here's the thing Black love is not a transaction. It's not something we earn by being perfect or by performing strength. It is a birthright.

It's the inheritance our ancestors prayed for. It's the legacy our children deserve to witness. It's the balm we keep trying to become for each other.

I know the statistics. I've heard the cynicism. I've seen the raised eyebrows when people talk about Black love as if it's a myth instead of a living, breathing reality happening in kitchens and bedrooms and front porches across this country.

But I refuse to let those narratives define us.

I refuse to believe that our love is more fragile, more fleeting, more fractured than anyone else's.

I refuse to accept that the wounds we've sustained individually and collectively make us less capable of creating and sustaining love that lasts.

Because I've seen otherwise.

I've seen Black couples who've weathered storms that would have destroyed others and still look at each other with tenderness in their eyes.

I've seen Black families create traditions of togetherness that defy every stereotype about absence and disconnection.

I've seen Black communities rally around love celebrating anniversaries, supporting new unions, honoring elders who've shown us what commitment looks like over decades.

And yes, we've hurt each other. Yes, we've misnamed and misunderstood. Yes, we've reenacted trauma we didn't create.

But we've also held space. We've also forgiven. We've also held each other through grief, through joy, through the middle of the night softness that nobody else ever sees.

That's what I believe in.

I believe in the love that says, "I know where you come from, and I still choose you." "I see what cracked you, and I still believe in your beauty." "I'm not here to fix you I'm here to love you through."

I believe in the kind of love that doesn't require perfection, just presence. The kind that understands that healing happens in relationship, not in isolation. The kind that knows that true intimacy isn't about never making mistakes, it's about how we repair when we do.

I believe in the kind of love that honors our history without being imprisoned by it. That acknowledges our wounds without being defined by them. That celebrates our resilience without demanding that we always be strong.

Beloved, we are allowed to believe in us. Even when the world doesn't. Even when the headlines don't. Even when the whispers try to tell us we're too broken, too complicated, too tired.

We are allowed to be soft with each other.

To laugh together again.

To say, "I'm sorry" and mean it.

To say, "I need you" and not flinch.

To say, "I'm healing" and be met with open arms instead of side eyes.

We are allowed to rebuild love not from obligation, but from truth. Not to prove something to the world, but because we remember who we are to each other.

You are not a threat to me. You are my mirror.

My witness.

My companion in the becoming.

And even with all the history personal and collective I still believe.

I believe that we can love without losing ourselves. I believe that we can grow old and grow whole. I believe that we can write new stories without erasing the old ones. I believe that what's broken can be blessed, if we handle it with care.

I believe that our love, Black love, is not just surviving, but evolving. Becoming something more nuanced, more honest, more equitable than what was modeled for us. Becoming something that honors both our individual journeys and our shared destiny.

I believe that we are writing a new chapter in an ancient story. That we are both inheritors and innovators of a love tradition that has sustained our people through unimaginable hardship.

And I believe that this evolution isn't just for us, it's for everyone who comes after us. For the children watching how we love, learning what's possible, internalizing that they too are worthy of love that doesn't diminish them.

So, this is my offering to you:

Let's keep believing.

Let's love anyway.

Let's rise anyway.

Let's hold each other in all the ways that matter, especially when it's not easy, especially when the world forgets how rare and real this kind of love truly is.

With faith in what's already sacred.

Always, Me

Chapter 9

Love Me Past the Masks and Muscle

Dear Beloved,

I know what the world asks of you.

To stand tall even when your knees are shaking. To flex when you really need to fall apart. To lead when you've never been led with care. To protect, while no one protects you.

And so, you learned to wear it well. That mask. That armor. That curated version of yourself that the world could accept, applaud, and depend on even if it meant hiding everything tender inside you.

But what I want you to know, what I need you to know, is that I don't want the mask. I want you.

I want the version of you who exhaled too deep when you didn't know anyone was watching. The one who second guesses himself in the dark but still shows up in the morning. The one who feels deeply but doesn't always know how to say so. The one who has scars emotional, spiritual, generational and still keeps trying to love through them.

That's the man I want to see. The one behind the performance.

I've watched you, Beloved, in those quiet moments when the world isn't looking. When you think no one can see. I've caught glimpses of what lives beneath the carefully constructed image you present, the vulnerability, the uncertainty, and the tenderness that you've been taught to hide.

I've seen how exhausting it is for you to maintain this facade. How the constant vigilance of appearing strong, appearing certain, appearing unaffected takes its toll. How you sometimes retreat into silence not because you have nothing to say, but because you're tired of saying only what others expect to hear.

This performance wasn't your choice. It was your survival.

In a world that criminalized your emotions, pathologized your anger, feared your grief, and misinterpreted your joy, you learned to curate yourself. To present only the parts deemed acceptable. To hide the rest behind walls, so thick that sometimes even you forget what's buried there.

Black men have been asked to be both invisible and hypervisible at the same time. To be strong but not threatening. To be successful but not too successful. To be present but not to take up too much space. To be emotional but only in ways that comfort rather than confront.

It's an impossible balance. A cruel contradiction. A game rigged from the start.

And still, you've played it. Because sometimes playing meant surviving. Sometimes the mask meant making it home at night. Sometimes the performance was the price of admission to spaces that should have welcomed all of you but only had room for parts.

I understand why the armor exists. I honor the protection it provides.

But Beloved, in this space between us, I'm asking for something different.

I'm asking for the man beneath the muscle. The truth behind the toughness. The heart behind the hardness.

I'm asking for the you that gets lost in music when no one's watching. The you that still feels wonder at a sunset or a child's laughter. The you that sometimes wants to be held without having to be strong first. The you that carries questions you've never felt safe enough to ask.

I want to love that man not because he's perfect, but because he's real.

I know it's scary to be seen. To let the mask slip. To stand without the armor you've worn for so long it sometimes feels like skin.

I know there's risk in vulnerability, especially for a Black man in a world that has used your openness against you, that has mistaken your emotion for weakness, your honesty for threat, your humanity for something less than.

But I am not the world, Beloved. I am not here to judge or diminish or control. I am here to witness. To receive. To hold space for all the parts of you, the strong and the soft, the certain and the seeking, the powerful and the tender.

I am here to love you past the masks and muscle, into the truth of who you are.

Because the real strength? It's not in never breaking. It's in allowing yourself to be broken open. To be seen in your wholeness cracks, questions, and all.

The real power? It's not in never needing. It's in being brave enough to name your needs, to reach for connection, to allow yourself to receive as generously as you give.

The real manhood? It's not in performance. It's in presence. In showing up authentically, even when authenticity means admitting you don't have all the answers. Even when it means letting tears fall. Even when it means saying "I'm scared" or "I don't know" or "I need help."

I've seen glimpses of this man in the way your voice softens when you speak of things you love. In the gentleness of your hands when you think no one's paying attention. In the depth of feeling that sometimes flashes across your face before the mask slides back into place.

That's the man I'm falling in love with. Not the image. Not the idea. But the complex, contradictory, beautifully human reality of you.

I know the unmasking isn't easy. I know it doesn't happen all at once.

Trust has been broken too many times. Vulnerability has been weaponized too often. Softness has been met with harm too frequently.

So, I'm not asking for immediate revelation. I'm not demanding that you shed decades of protective layers overnight.

I'm simply creating space for the unfolding. For the slow, sacred revelation of your truest self. For the gradual lowering of defenses as you learn that, with me, your wholeness is not just accepted but celebrated.

And in that space, I promise this:

I will not use your openness against you. I will not mistake your emotion for weakness. I will not demand performance as the price of my presence.

I will meet your truth with tenderness. I will hold your questions without rushing to answers. I will witness your unfolding without demanding it happen on my timeline.

Because I don't want to love the mask, Beloved. I don't want to love the muscle. I don't want to love the man the world told you to be.

I want to love you in all your complexity, all your contradiction, all your becoming.

The you who sometimes needs to be held. The you who sometimes doesn't have the words. The you who sometimes feels lost but keeps going anyway. The you who carries both strength and softness, both power and pain, both certainty and doubt.

That's the love that will sustain us not one built on performance or pretense, but on the revolutionary act of being fully seen and still chosen. Of being known in your entirety and still cherished. Of being human, with all the mess and magic that entails, and still considered worthy.

So, whenever you're ready, Beloved whether it's today or tomorrow or in the quiet moments that stretch between I'm here.

Not for the mask. Not for the muscle. But for the man. The real one. The whole one. The one I choose, again and again, even as he's still becoming.

With love that sees beyond the surface.

Always, Me

Chapter 10

Beloved, You Were Never My Enemy

Dear Beloved,

Somewhere along the way, we forgot.

We forgot that we were on the same team. We forgot that your victory was never my loss. We forgot that being loved and being right are not the same thing.

And in that forgetting, something sacred broke.

We began to guard instead of give. We began to defend instead of disclose. We began to hurt each other not because we stopped caring, but because we didn't know how to stop protecting ourselves.

And now here we are two people who love each other but sometimes act like adversaries. Two people who have been trained by this world to see each other through the lens of suspicion, scorekeeping, and silence.

But Beloved, I need to say this: You were never my enemy.

Not when your words came out wrong.

Not when mine did too.

Not when we built distance out of misunderstanding, or armor out of unspoken grief.

You were never the threat.

The enemy was the wound. The enemy was the story we inherited that said connection required control. The enemy was the noise that told us love had to be earned, defended, or withheld.

But not you. Never you.

We may have hurt each other. But we didn't start that hurt.

We walked into this with bags we didn't pack. We carried the weight of generations who never learned to say, "I'm scared," so they said, "I'm fine." We inherited the broken bones of Black love that was stretched thin by systems and shame, by poverty and patriarchy, by racism and roles we never agreed to play.

But Beloved, just because we inherited it doesn't mean we have to live in it.

We can put the weapons down. We can stop treating every disagreement like a war. We can stop waiting for the other to flinch first, fold first, fail first.

You are not my opponent. You are not my battlefield.

I think about how we got here sometimes. How the world taught us to be suspicious of each other's intentions. How we learned to read threats into neutral expressions, to assume the worst about each other's silences, to prepare for abandonment even in the midst of commitment.

These weren't lessons we chose. They were survival mechanisms passed down through generations of Black folks who had to be vigilant just to stay alive. Who had to anticipate harm before it arrived. Who had to protect themselves in a world that offered little protection.

And those mechanisms served a purpose. They kept our ancestors alert to danger. They helped them navigate hostile environments. They created a kind of hyperawareness that, in many contexts, was necessary.

But between us? In this sacred space of love and partnership? Those same mechanisms become barriers. They keep us from the very connection we're seeking. They turn potential allies into perceived threats.

I see it in the way we sometimes brace for impact before difficult conversations. In the way we gather evidence for our positions instead of listening for understanding. In the way we sometimes speak to wound rather than to heal, because somewhere along the way, we learned that offense was the best defense.

But what if we're defending against the wrong thing?

What if the real threat isn't each other, but the patterns we've inherited? The fear that love won't last. The belief that vulnerability equals weakness. The idea that someone must win and someone must lose.

These are the true enemies, not you, not me, but the narratives that position us against each other instead of beside each other.

Our ancestors survived not just through vigilance, but through solidarity. How they built community in the face of forces that tried to divide them. How they found ways to love and support each other even when the world gave them every reason to distrust.

That legacy lives in us too, Beloved. That capacity for connection. That ability to see beyond the surface to the soul beneath. That wisdom that knows true safety isn't found in walls, but in bridges.

We just have to remember.

We have to remember that your pain and my pain may look different, may express differently, may need different things but they're not in competition. They're both valid. They both deserve care.

We have to remember that your healing and my healing are interconnected. That when you thrive, I benefit. That when I'm whole, you're supported. That our well-being was never meant to be a zero-sum game.

We have to remember that the systems that tried to break us, that separated families, that criminalized Black love, that created economic conditions that strained relationships; those systems win when we turn on each other. They win when we forget our shared humanity and shared struggle.

But we don't have to give them that victory.

We can choose a different path.

We can choose to see disagreement not as betrayal, but as an opportunity to understand each other more deeply. To learn the contours of each other's hearts. To grow in our capacity to hold complexity.

We can choose to approach conflict not as combat, but as collaboration; two people working together to solve a shared problem, even when that problem is between us.

We can choose to remember, even in our most wounded moments, that we are not each other's enemies. That the person standing across from us, even in anger or hurt, is still the same person we've chosen, still the same soul we've recognized as kindred.

This isn't easy work, Beloved. It goes against everything we've been taught about self-protection. It requires us to stay open when every instinct says to close. To reach when we want to retreat. To speak truth when silence feels safer.

But I believe we're capable of it.

I believe we can unlearn the habits of opposition and relearn the art of alliance. I believe we can heal the rifts not by ignoring them, but by crossing them again and again, with patience and persistence. I believe we can create a love that isn't defined by the wounds of our past, but by the vision of our future.

You are not my enemy. You are not the enemy of my joy, my healing, my wholeness.

You are my kin. My co-conspirator in softness.

My mirror.

My muse.

My reminder that love is still possible, even in the rubble.

We have to choose a new way. A way that doesn't mean shrinking ourselves just to keep the peace. A way that doesn't mean shouting just to feel heard. A way that doesn't mean loving at the cost of self, but rather loving with self, together.

Because I don't want to win. I want to we.

I want a love that doesn't score points but builds bridges. A love that pauses when things get loud and says, "Let's try that again." A love that says, "I see your wound, and I will not use it against you."

I want to fight with you, not against you.

And I know it takes time. I know it takes trust. I know it takes unlearning things we didn't even know were living inside of us.

But I believe in us. Not a fantasy version. Not a perfect, unshaken pair. But a real us; messy, healing, honest.

So let me say it again, clearly, slowly, and with love: You were never my enemy. Not even in the argument. Not even in the silence. Not even when we were both too tired to try.

You are not the fight. You are the reason I fight for softness, for clarity, for connection, for healing.

So, let's stop drawing lines between us. Let's draw circles instead. Circles of grace. Circles of return. Circles of peace.

Come sit beside me, not across from me. Let's face the world together. Let's build something the system can't steal. Let's remember that our survival is linked, and our joy is too.

With arms uncrossed and heart unguarded.

Always, Me

Chapter 11

Let's Grow Old in Joy, Not Just Survival

Dear Beloved,

We've learned how to survive. That much is clear.

We know how to carry the weight, hold the line, stay when it's hard, and fight when we need to. We've mastered endurance because we had to.

But I want more for us now.

I don't just want to grow old with you I want to grow whole. I want to grow with laughter in our lungs and light in our bones. I want a life that feels less like a battlefield and more like a front porch. One where joy isn't rare, but rhythmic. Where peace isn't earned through pain but held like a birthright.

Because somewhere along the way, we got good at managing each other... but forgot how to delight in each other. We started doing love like a job clocking in, checking boxes, waiting for retirement.

But Beloved, I want us to do love like art. Messy. Creative. Sacred. Ongoing.

I want us to remember why we reached for each other in the first place. Not because we were perfect. Not because we had all the answers. But because our souls felt safe in one another's presence.

That kind of love deserves more than survival. It deserves joy.

I think about our people sometimes; how joy has always been an act of resistance for us. How even in the darkest chapters of our history, Black folks found ways to celebrate, to create beauty, to laugh deep from the belly. Our ancestors understood that survival alone wasn't enough that without joy, without pleasure, without moments of sweetness, survival was just another kind of death.

They knew something we sometimes forget; that joy isn't frivolous. It's essential. It's the fuel that keeps us going when the road gets rough. It's the light that guides us home when the path seems dark. It's the reminder that we are more than our struggles, more than our pain, more than our resilience.

We are also worthy of delight.

I see how hard you've worked, Beloved. How you've shouldered burdens without complaint. How you've pushed through exhaustion, through doubt, through fear, just to make sure everyone else was taken care of. How you've treated joy as something to be earned rather than embraced, as a luxury rather than a necessity.

But what if joy isn't the reward for surviving? What if it's what makes survival possible in the first place?

I know joy takes work. Especially when we're tired. Especially when the world pulls us in every direction and trauma tells us, it's safer not to hope.

But joy is worth fighting for.

Not the loud kind, not the performative kind but the kind that shows up when you're folding laundry and our song comes on, and we both stop just to dance barefoot in the kitchen.

I want that kind of joy. Quiet. Consistent. Real.

I want the joy that lingers after hard conversations. The kind that says, "We're still here. Still choosing each other. Still building."

I want the joy that lives in the mundane moments passing you your coffee the way you like it, catching your eye across the room, smiling because you still look like home to me.

I've caught glimpses of this joy in you in the way your face softens when you talk about things you love. In the sound of your laughter when it's genuine, not performed. In the moments when you let yourself play without worrying about looking dignified or responsible or strong.

In those moments, I see the boy you once were curious, open hearted, unafraid to feel deeply. The boy who hadn't yet learned that Black men aren't supposed to be too happy, too expressive, too free. The boy who knew how to receive joy without questioning whether he deserved it.

That boy is still in you, Beloved. Still waiting for permission to emerge. Still hoping for spaces where his enthusiasm won't be misread as aggression, his expressiveness won't be labeled as too much, his joy won't be seen as a threat.

I want to create that space with you. A sanctuary for your joy. A home where your laughter can echo without restraint. A relationship where pleasure isn't something you have to earn, but something you're entitled to by virtue of being human.

Let's create that together.

Let's age in intimacy not just in years, but in knowing. Let's become so familiar with each other's hearts that even our silence feels like a love song.

And yes, we'll still have valleys. But let's not make the valley our address.

Let's climb. Let's rise. Let's laugh more than we argue. Let's hold hands in public and pray together in private. Let's slow dance even when our knees start to creak.

I think about growing old with you, and I don't picture perfection. I don't imagine a life without challenges or conflicts or hard days. But I do envision a life where joy is our compass, not just an occasional destination. Where we've learned to navigate the rough waters without forgetting how to float, how to play, how to delight in the journey itself.

I picture us with gray hair and laugh lines, sitting on a porch swing, watching the world go by. I picture us telling stories that start with "Remember when..." and end with the kind of laughter that comes from shared history, shared struggle, shared triumph. I picture us holding hands not just out of habit, but out of choice, still choosing each other, still finding wonder in the familiar landscape of each other's souls.

That's the kind of aging I want for us. Not just accumulating years, but accumulating moments of tenderness, of silliness, of awe. Not just enduring but enjoying. Not just making it through but making it beautiful.

Because the goal is not just longevity, it's legacy.

Let our love be a soft place for us, and a blueprint for those coming behind us. Let the children, the neighbors, the community say, "Look how they kept choosing. Look how they loved with joy still on their faces."

We've already proven that we can survive. Now let's show the world and ourselves that we can thrive.

I know this isn't simple. I know that for many Black men, joy has been a luxury rarely afforded. I know that the world has given you plenty of reasons to be guarded, to be serious, to focus on protection rather than pleasure.

I know that sometimes joy feels risky, like letting your guard down in a world that hasn't always been safe for your heart, your body, and your spirit.

But I also know this: joy is your birthright. Not a privilege to be earned, but an inheritance to be claimed. Not a distraction from the serious work of living, but the very purpose of it.

And I want to be your companion in reclaiming that inheritance. In remembering how to play without purpose, laugh without restraint, love without fear. In building a life where joy isn't the exception, but the rule.

Beloved, I want a soft old age with you.

I want us sitting on a porch, watching the sky change colors, reminiscing about how we made it through and how we kept laughing anyway.

I want to hold your hand when it's wrinkled, when our steps are slower, when our bodies have changed but our hearts still remember the rhythm of love that brought us here.

Let's build that life. One where joy is not an occasional visitor, but a permanent resident. One where love doesn't just last, it lives.

With hope for a future held in joy.

Always, Me

Chapter 12

Even with Cracked Wings, I Chose You

Dear Beloved,

I didn't choose you because you were perfect.

I didn't choose you because you always had the right words, or made the right moves, or carried your pain like it didn't weigh anything.

I chose you because even when you were hurting, you still showed up. Because even when the world tried to harden you, you stayed soft in the places that mattered most.

I saw the cracks.

Not just in your past, but in your present. In the way your voice sometimes caught mid-sentence. In the way you flinched when love came too close. In the way you braced for rejection even as you reached for connection.

And still I chose you.

Not out of pity. Not to fix you. Not to be your savior.

But to be your witness. Your partner. Your peace.

Because your cracks? They didn't scare me. They reminded me of my own.

See, I wasn't looking for perfection, I was looking for presence. I wasn't asking for polished, I was asking for real. And you gave me that, even if you didn't always know how.

I chose you because beneath the armor, I saw tenderness. Beneath the silence, I heard the ache. Beneath the survival, I felt the longing.

And I wanted to love that man. The one behind the mask. The one who stayed when it would have been easier to leave. The one who held on, even when he didn't know what healing would look like.

I remember the first time I truly saw you not the version you present to the world, but the soul beneath the surface. How your eyes held stories you hadn't yet found words for. How your hands, strong as they were, sometimes trembled when you reached for connection. How your laughter, when it was real, came from somewhere deep and unguarded.

In those moments of unfiltered humanity, I recognized something familiar. Something that resonated with my own journey of breaking and becoming. Something that whispered, "Here is someone who knows what it means to fall and rise, to hurt and heal, to doubt and still dare to believe."

This world teaches us to hide our wounds, to cover our scars, to pretend we've never been broken. It tells us that worthiness comes from wholeness, that love must be earned through perfection. It sells us the myth that the most desirable people are the ones who've never struggled, never questioned, never cracked under the weight of living.

But Beloved, that was never the truth.

The most beautiful souls I've known are the ones who've been shattered and still chose to love. The ones who've faced their own darkness and still chose to bring light. The ones who've been disappointed again and again and still chose to hope.

You are one of those souls.

Your journey hasn't been smooth or straight. You've taken detours through doubt, made stops in sorrow, gotten lost in landscapes of loss. You've carried burdens that weren't yours to bear, fought battles that weren't yours to fight, endured pain that wasn't yours to feel.

And yes, those experiences left marks. Cracks in the foundation. Fractures in the facade. Places where the light gets in, but also places where the rain seeps through.

Beloved, choosing you wasn't a romantic gesture. It was a radical one. A sacred one.

Because choosing you meant choosing us. Choosing the long road of unlearning and becoming. Choosing to return, again and again, when everything in the world said to run. Choosing to hold space when it hurts, to tell the truth when it trembled, to forgive when it felt like fire.

It meant choosing a love that doesn't demand perfection but invites authenticity. A love that doesn't require you to hide your wounds but offers to sit beside them. A love that doesn't expect you to have all the answers but promises to ask the questions with you.

I think about the narratives we've been fed about Black love how it's often portrayed as either idealized or impossible. How rarely we see stories that honor the complexity, the struggle, and the beauty of two people choosing each other not despite their brokenness, but with full awareness of it.

How rarely we see Black men loved not for their strength alone, but for their vulnerability. Not for their resilience alone, but for their tenderness. Not for what they can provide or protect, but for who they are in their fullness of questions, fears, dreams, and all.

I wanted to write a different story with you. One that acknowledges the cracks but doesn't define us by them. One that honors the journey without pretending the path has been easy. One that celebrates the choosing not once, but again and again, day after day, in the face of everything that would pull us apart.

And if I could go back to the moment when I first saw you clearly, not just with my eyes, but with my soul, I'd choose you all over again.

Even with the cracks. Even with the scars. Even with the fear that sometimes stands in the way of your softness.

Because the cracks didn't diminish your worth. They revealed your depth.

You are not some broken thing I settled for. You are the beauty I recognized because I've broken, too. And that's what makes this real.

There's a Japanese art form called kintsugi, where broken pottery is repaired with gold. The philosophy behind it is that breakage and repair are part of the history of an object, not something to disguise or hide. The cracks are illuminated, honored, transformed from damage to distinction.

That's how I see you, Beloved. Not as someone whose worth is diminished by life's fractures, but as someone whose beauty is illuminated by them. The places where you've been broken and mended, where you've fallen and risen, where you've doubted and still chosen to believe these aren't flaws to be hidden. They're evidence of a life fully lived, a heart fully engaged, and a soul fully committed to growth.

We were never meant to save each other. We were meant to see each other. To witness the becoming. To hold one another as we grew wings from the rubble.

I know there have been times when the weight felt too heavy. When the path seemed too steep. When the hurt ran too deep. Times when you questioned whether you were worthy of love, whether healing was possible, whether joy could ever be more than a fleeting visitor.

There were days I almost forgot how to stay soft. But then I'd remember how you reached for me clumsily, maybe, but courageously. And I'd soften again. I'd breathe again. I'd choose again.

Because love is not always loud. Sometimes it's just a quiet return. A leaning in. A hand held in the dark. A whispered, "I'm still here."

That's the kind of love that lasts. Not the kind that never faces challenges, but the kind that faces them together. Not the kind that never questions, but the kind that stays even when the questions have no easy answers. Not the kind that never cracks, but the kind that knows how to rebuild, again and again, with patience and presence.

Beloved, I wrote these letters not just for you, but to you. So, you'd know:

You were always worthy.

Even when you doubted.

Even when you disappeared for a while.

Even when your wings didn't look like anyone else's.

You were still flying. Maybe low. Maybe slow. But still in the air. Still rising.

And now, as we close this chapter not the story, just the page I want you to carry this truth with you like a compass:

You are not the sum of your mistakes. You are not the myth they made of you. You are not too much, too late, too far gone.

You are worthy. You are becoming. You are loved.

And even with cracked wings... I chose you.

With every beat of this imperfect, persistent, powerful love.

Always, Me

Chapter 13

The Dreams You Set Aside

Dear Beloved,

I see them sometimes those dreams you tucked away.

They flicker in your eyes when you watch certain films. They hide in the corners of your smile when you hear stories of roads not taken. They live in the gentle way your hands move when you speak of what might have been.

Those dreams you set aside.

Not abandoned, not forgotten, just carefully folded and placed on a shelf while you handled what needed handling. While you became the man they said you needed to be: provider, protector, present. The one who makes sure everyone else's dreams have room to breathe.

I know you had to make choices. Hard ones. Practical ones. Necessary ones.

The scholarship you declined because your family needed you close. The creative path you diverted from because it didn't promise stability. The risks you couldn't take because too many people were depending on your certainty.

This world has asked Black men to trade passion for practicality, to exchange exploration for expectation, to substitute survival for self-expression. It has measured your worth by what you produce, not by what you dream. By what you provide, not by what you imagine.

And you did what you had to do.

You chose responsibility.

You chose family.

You chose the known path over the uncertain one.

You chose to be the rock when others needed something solid to stand on.

I honor those choices, Beloved. I see the sacrifice in them. I recognize the love embedded in each decision to set your own longings aside.

But I also want to whisper something to that part of you that still remembers what it wanted before the world told you what you should want:

Those dreams weren't frivolous. They weren't childish. They weren't luxuries you didn't deserve.

They were glimpses of your soul's true shape. They were echoes of your authentic voice. They were maps to parts of yourself you haven't fully explored.

And they're still there.

Maybe altered by time. Maybe transformed by experience. Maybe waiting to be reimagined in ways that honor who you've become. But still there still alive, still yours to reclaim.

I see how you sometimes dismiss them now. How you wave them away with a laugh or a shrug. "That was a long time ago," you say. Or, "That's not practical." Or, "I'm too old for that now."

But Beloved, dreams don't have expiration dates. Purpose doesn't have a timeline. Passion doesn't belong only to the young.

Some of the most beautiful creations have come from those who found their way back to abandoned dreams in the middle or latter chapters of their lives. Some of the most powerful contributions have emerged from people who finally gave themselves permission to pursue what called to them, even after decades of deferral.

I'm not suggesting you abandon your responsibilities or upend everything you've built. I'm not asking you to trade security for recklessness or stability for chaos.

I'm simply inviting you to make a little space even if it's just in the quiet corners of your days for those dreams you set aside. To acknowledge them. To honor them. To consider whether some small seed of them might still be planted and nurtured, even in the life you now lead.

What if that music you used to make could find its way back into your evenings? What if that book you wanted to write could begin as a few sentences scribbled before bed? What if that skill you longed to master could be approached one small lesson at a time? What if that place you wanted to see could become next year's destination?

Your dreams matter, Beloved. Not just the ones that align with your roles and responsibilities. Not just the ones that serve others. But the ones that serve your soul. The ones that light you up from within. The ones that remind you that before you were anyone else's anything, you were a universe of possibilities.

I know the weight of expectation you carry. The pressure to be the strong one, the stable one, the one who sacrifices without complaint. I know how the narrative of the selfless Black man the one who puts everyone else first has been both a source of pride and a heavy burden.

But what if your joy is also a gift to those you love? What if pursuing your passion creates more possibilities, not less, for those who depend on you? What if reclaiming your dreams shows the next generation that duty and desire don't have to be enemies?

I believe there's room for both responsibility and dreams. For commitment and creativity. For being there for others and being true to yourself.

I believe that the man who finds his way back to his own heart has even more to offer those he loves. That the man who honors his own dreams teaches others how to honor theirs. That the man who gives himself permission to pursue passion gives others permission to do the same.

So, this letter is an invitation, Beloved. An invitation to dust off those dreams you set aside. To hold them up to the light. To see which ones still resonate, which ones still call to you, which ones still feel like home.

It's an invitation to consider what small step you might take, not someday, but today toward something that makes your soul sing. Something that reconnects you to the boy who believed anything was possible. Something that honors not just what you can do or provide, but who you are at your core.

Because you deserve a life that includes not just duty, but delight. Not just service, but self-expression. Not just responsibility, but joy.

Those dreams you set aside?

They're still yours to claim.

Still, yours to reshape.

Still, yours to pursue not instead of the life you've built, but alongside it. As part of a fuller, richer expression of who you are and who you're still becoming.

I see them, Beloved. I honor them. And I'll make space for them to breathe whenever you're ready to let them out into the light again.

With belief in all you are and all you're yet to be.

Always, Me

Chapter 14

When the World Misreads Your Silence

Dear Beloved,

Your silence speaks volumes, but the world rarely knows how to listen.

I've watched it happen how your thoughtful pause gets labeled as anger. How your quiet contemplation is mistaken for disengagement. How your measured response is interpreted as coldness. How your internal processing is read as indifference.

The world has created so many false narratives around Black men's silence.

They see threat where there is reflection. They see withdrawal where there is wisdom gathering. They see stubbornness where there is careful consideration. They see absence where there is simply a different kind of presence.

But I see the truth of your silence.

I see how you retreat into quiet not to disconnect, but to protect the tenderness that lives inside you. How you pause not because you don't care, but because you care enough to find the right words. How you step back not to disengage, but to gain perspective before responding.

Your silence is not empty. It's full of everything you're processing, everything you're feeling, everything you're carefully considering before you speak it into existence.

I know the weight of being constantly misread. The exhaustion of having your intentions twisted, your thoughtfulness misinterpreted, your natural way of being in the world treated as a problem to be solved rather than a perspective to be understood.

I know how it feels to be told directly or indirectly that your natural rhythm of communication is wrong. Too slow. Too measured. Too contained. I know the pressure to perform extroversion, to fill every silence, to process out loud just to make others comfortable with your presence.

But Beloved, your silence is sacred.

It's the space where you integrate experience. It's the moment where wisdom forms. It's the pause where truth crystallizes. It's the breath between reaction and response.

In a world that demands immediate answers, constant engagement, and performative expression, your ability to be still, to reflect, to consider deeply before speaking is not a flaw, it's a gift. A rare and necessary counterbalance to a culture of hasty words and unexamined reactions.

For our ancestors silence was often survival. How they learned to hold their tongues in hostile environments, to communicate through glances and gestures, to say one thing with their mouths and another with their eyes. How they passed down this ability to navigate multiple layers of meaning, to speak volumes without saying a word.

That legacy lives in you. That depth. That discernment. That ability to communicate beyond language, to read the unspoken, to hear what isn't being said.

But I also know that this gift comes with a cost.

The cost of being misunderstood.

The cost of having your silence filled with other people's projections.

The cost of being labeled: distant, difficult, disinterested, dangerous.

I've seen how these misreadings wound you. How they create distance where there could be connection. How they force you to either abandon your natural way of being or accept being perpetually misinterpreted.

It's an impossible choice that no one should have to make.

So, I want to say this clearly: Your silence is valid. Your internal processing is valuable. Your thoughtful pauses are powerful. Your measured responses are meaningful.

You don't need to perform extroversion to be worthy of understanding. You don't need to process out loud to be engaged. You don't need to fill every silence to be present.

What you need; what we all need is the space to be authentic. To communicate in ways that honor our natural rhythms. To be understood rather than constantly translated.

I promise to create that space with you. To listen not just to your words, but to your silence. To understand that your quiet is not an absence but presence in a different form. To give you room to process in your own way, at your own pace, without demanding performance or immediate response.

And I want to encourage you to claim that space more broadly. To gently educate those who misread you. To correct misinterpretations when it feels safe to do so. To find communities and relationships where your natural way of communicating is valued rather than problematized.

Because your voice matters not just when it's loud, but when it's soft. Not just when it's immediate, but when it's measured. Not just when it conforms to others' expectations, but when it expresses your authentic self.

The world needs your particular kind of communication.

Your thoughtfulness.

Your depth.

Your ability to pause and consider before speaking.

Your gift for saying much with few words.

In a culture of noise, your silence is revolutionary. In a world of hasty reactions, your reflection is radical. In a society that fears pauses, your comfort with quiet is profound.

I've noticed how people rush to fill the spaces you create. How your silence makes them uncomfortable, makes them babble and overexplain. How they mistake your listening for judgment, your observation for criticism, your stillness for stonewalling.

They don't understand that sometimes, your silence is a gift. An offering of space where truth can emerge without pressure. A moment of genuine attention in a world of distraction. A pause that honors the weight of what's being discussed rather than rushing past it.

They don't see how your silence can be an act of care. How you choose your words carefully not to manipulate or minimize, but to ensure they carry the truth you intend. How you listen fully before responding, giving others the rare gift of being completely heard.

They don't recognize how your silence can be self-protection in spaces that have weaponized your words, twisted your meanings, and used your vulnerability against you. How sometimes staying quiet is not withdrawal, but wisdom is the discernment to know when a space isn't safe for your voice.

So, take up space with your silence, Beloved. Let it expand and contract according to your needs, not others' comfort. Let it serve as boundary and as bridge, as shield and as connection, as rest and as resistance.

Your silence is not something to overcome or fix or apologize for. It's something to honor.

To understand.

To appreciate. It's part of the beautiful, complex language that is uniquely yours.

And I am listening not just to what you say, but to all the ways you communicate beyond words. To the rhythm of your presence. To the eloquence of your pauses. To the poetry of your silence.

I hear you, Beloved. All of you. Even especially in the quiet.

With deep listening and patient presence.

Always, Me

Chapter 15

Your Body Carries Wisdom

Dear Beloved,

Your body has been trying to tell you something.

I've noticed it in the tension that gathers at the base of your neck after certain conversations. In the way your shoulders rise toward your ears when you're bracing for impact. In the headaches that come when you've been holding too much for too long. In the exhaustion that settles into your bones on Sunday evenings.

Your body carries wisdom that your mind sometimes ignores.

For generations, Black men have been taught to push through. To override the body's signals. To ignore pain. To keep going, keep providing, keep protecting even when your physical form is begging for rest, for relief, for attention.

"Mind over matter," they told you. "No pain, no gain," they said. "Man up," they insisted when your body tried to speak.

And so, you learned to silence your own flesh. To treat your body as a machine rather than a messenger. To wear exhaustion like a badge of honor rather than a warning sign.

But Beloved, your body is speaking a language of profound wisdom.

It knows what your conscious mind sometimes forgets that you are not invincible. That you are not made of steel. That you are a living, breathing organism that requires care, attention, and rest to thrive.

When your jaw clenches at night, it's telling you about the words you've swallowed during the day. When your lower back aches, it's reminding you of the burdens you've been carrying without support. When your stomach knots, it's speaking of fears your voice hasn't named. When fatigue overwhelms you after certain interactions, it's revealing which relationships drain rather than sustain you.

These aren't weaknesses, Beloved. They're intelligence. Your body's brilliant system of alerts and alarms, designed to protect you, to guide you, to help you navigate this complex world with greater awareness.

I think about the generational weight your body carries. The trauma that lives not just in memory, but in muscle. The vigilance that was passed down as survival. The tension that became so normal you stopped noticing it was there.

Research tells us now, what our ancestors knew intuitively that trauma doesn't just live in the mind. It lives in the body. It shapes how we hold ourselves, how we breathe, and how we move through the world. It creates patterns of tension and release, of bracing and collapse, that become so familiar we mistake them for who we are.

But they are not who you are, Beloved. They are what happened to you. What happened to those who came before you. What happened in a world that demanded Black men be both hypervisible and invisible, both superhuman and less than human.

Your body remembers everything, the direct wounds and the witnessed ones. The personal hurts and the collective traumas. The times you were treated as a threat simply for existing in your skin. The times you had to make yourself smaller, quieter, less present just to move through certain spaces safely.

It remembers, and it responds with tension, with vigilance, with a constant readiness for danger that exhausts you even when you're "at rest."

This is not your imagination. This is not weakness. This is your body's profound intelligence, its attempt to keep you safe in a world that has often been unsafe for Black men.

But safety that comes at the cost of constant vigilance is not truly safety at all. Protection that requires perpetual armoring eventually becomes its own kind of prison.

What would it mean to begin listening to your body's wisdom in a new way? Not to override its signals, but to receive them as information. Not to push through pain, but to understand what it's trying to tell you. Not to wear exhaustion as a badge of honor, but to recognize it as a call for the rest you deeply deserve.

What would it mean to treat your physical form not as a machine to be pushed or a resource to be depleted, but as a sacred vessel deserving of care, of tenderness, of attention?

I know this isn't simple. I know that for many Black men, the luxury of rest has been exactly that a luxury, not a given. I know that systems of oppression have relied on extracting labor from Black bodies while denying them care. I know that even now, your pain is often minimized, your fatigue often dismissed, your need for rest is often treated as laziness rather than necessity.

But your body deserves better. You deserve better.

You deserve to breathe fully, not in the shallow way that comes with constant vigilance. You deserve to sleep deeply, not in the fitful way that comes with unprocessed stress. You deserve to move freely, not in the constrained way that comes with perpetual armoring. You deserve to rest completely, not in the partial way that comes with always being on alert.

Your body is not just a vehicle to carry you through life or a tool to accomplish tasks. It is life itself. It is the physical expression of your spirit, the tangible form of your soul, the home in which you experience this precious existence.

And it has been carrying so much not just your individual burdens, but the weight of expectations, stereotypes, historical trauma, daily microaggressions, constant code switching, perpetual vigilance.

No wonder you're tired, Beloved. No wonder your shoulders ache. No wonder sleep sometimes eludes you. No wonder certain spaces leave you drained even when nothing overtly negative has occurred.

Your body knows. It has always known. It has been trying to tell you what your mind has been trained to ignore that you need rest. That you need care. That you need spaces where you can fully exhale, where your nervous system can remember what safety feels like, where your muscles can release the tension they've been holding for so long.

This isn't self-indulgence. This is self-preservation. This is wisdom. This is honoring the vessel that carries your brilliant mind, your beautiful spirit, and your precious life.

So, I invite you, Beloved, to begin a new relationship with your body. To listen to its signals, not as inconveniences to be overcome, but as wisdom to be heeded. To treat pain not as weakness, but as information. To view rest not as luxury, but as necessity.

Start small if you need to. A few deep breaths when you notice tension rising. A moment to check in with your body before you override its signals. A commitment to rest before exhaustion forces it upon you. A willingness to say "no" to demands that would deplete you beyond recovery.

Your body has been speaking to you all along. It has been trying to guide you toward balance, toward wholeness, toward a way of being that honors your humanity rather than sacrificing it on the altar of productivity or strength or service.

It's time to listen, Beloved. Time to receive the wisdom your body has been offering. Time to honor the physical form that has carried you through so much with such resilience.

Your body is not separate from your spirit. Your physical well-being is not disconnected from your emotional health. Your flesh and blood and bone are not just containers for your essence they are expressions of it.

So, tend to your body with the same care you would offer your most precious relationships. Listen to it with the same attention you would give your most trusted advisor. Honor it with the same reverence you would show your most sacred beliefs.

Because your body carries wisdom that the world desperately needs wisdom about pace, about rhythm, about the true meaning of strength. Wisdom that comes not from pushing beyond limits, but from living within the natural cycles of effort and rest, of giving and receiving, of doing and being.

Your body knows, Beloved. It has always known. And when you listen, truly listen to what it's telling you, you reclaim not just your physical well-being, but your birthright to exist as a whole, integrated being. Not a mind separate from a body, but a complete, embodied soul.

With reverence for the wisdom your body carries.

Always, Me

Chapter 16

The Courage in Your Gentleness

Dear Beloved,

There is a particular kind of courage I've witnessed in you, one that rarely gets celebrated, rarely gets named for the revolutionary act it truly is.

It's the courage of your gentleness.

In a world that has tried to convince you that strength looks like hardness, like dominance, like emotional distance you have dared, in your quiet moments, to be soft. To be tender. To be gentle in ways that defy everything you were taught about Black manhood.

I've seen it in the way your voice changes when you speak to children dropping to a cadence that invites rather than commands. I've noticed how your hands, capable of such strength, know instinctively how to touch with delicacy when something is fragile. I've witnessed how you listen, truly listen, when someone shares their pain, without rushing to fix or dismiss or compete.

These aren't small things, Beloved. These are acts of profound courage.

Because gentleness, for a Black man, has never been neutral. It has been dangerous. It has been misread as weakness. It has been treated as vulnerability to be exploited rather than strength to be honored. It has been systematically discouraged, from the playground to the boardroom, from the street corner to the family dinner table.

"Don't be soft," they told you. "Toughen up," they insisted. "Real men don't show tenderness," they claimed.

And beneath these messages was an unspoken truth: that in a world that already sees Black men as threats, your gentleness might not be enough to protect you. That in a society that has criminalized your very existence, your softness might be used against you. That in a culture that expects you to be either dangerous or subservient, your tenderness might make you a target.

So, you learned, as so many Black men have, to reserve your gentleness for private spaces. To show it only to those who had earned your deepest trust. To guard it like the precious resource it is.

But Beloved, I want you to know: I see the courage in your gentleness. I recognize the revolutionary power in your tenderness. I honor the strength it takes to remain soft in a world that has given you every reason to harden.

Because true power isn't found in domination. It's found in the capacity to be gentle when gentleness is called for. To be tender when tenderness is needed. To touch lightly when a situation requires delicacy rather than force.

Our ancestors survived not just through resistance, but through tenderness. How they created rituals of care in the midst of unspeakable cruelty. How they passed down lullabies and healing practices and gentle ways of being with one another, even when the world showed them no gentleness in return.

That legacy lives in you. That capacity to create softness in a hard world. That ability to offer tenderness even when you've been shown so little of it yourself. That gift of gentle presence; that creates safety for those around you.

It's a different kind of strength than the world typically celebrates in Black men. It doesn't look like physical dominance or emotional stoicism or aggressive success. It looks like the way you kneel to meet a child at eye level. The way you speak words of comfort without minimizing someone's pain. The way you hold space for others' vulnerability without making them feel weak for needing that space.

This gentleness is not weakness, Beloved. It is power of the most profound kind.

It's the power to heal rather than harm. It's the power to connect rather than control. It's the power to nurture growth rather than force compliance. It's the power to create safety rather than fear.

And it takes immense courage to express this kind of power in a world that has tried to convince you that your worth as a man especially as a Black man is tied to how feared you are, how little you need, how rarely you show anything that could be mistaken for vulnerability.

I've watched you navigate this contradiction; how to be both strong and gentle in a world that insists these qualities are opposed. How to be both protective and tender in a society that recognizes only the former as masculine. How to be both powerful and nurturing in a culture that has tried to separate these aspects of your humanity.

It's a delicate balance, and you walk it with such grace. Such intention. Such courage.

Because it is courage, Beloved, to reclaim the fullness of your humanity in a world that has tried to reduce you to stereotypes. It is courage to express tenderness when you've been taught that tenderness makes you a target. It is courage to remain gentle when gentleness has been used against you.

I think about the cost of this courage and how exhausting it must be to constantly navigate when it's safe to be soft and when the armor must come back on. How confusing it must be to receive mixed messages about your gentleness valued in some contexts, penalized in others. How painful it must be to have this essential part of yourself misunderstood, dismissed, or exploited.

And still, you choose gentleness. Still, you offer tenderness. Still, you remain soft in the places that matter most.

That's not just strength, Beloved. That's revolution.

Because every time you choose gentleness over hardness, tenderness over detachment, vulnerability over armor, you are rewriting the narrative about Black manhood. You are expanding the possibilities for those who come after you. You are creating space for a more complete, more authentic expression of what it means to be both Black and male in this world.

You are showing that true power doesn't diminish others, it elevates them. That true strength isn't about how much you can dominate it's about how deeply you can connect. That true courage isn't found in never being vulnerable, it's found in being vulnerable even when vulnerability comes with risk.

I want you to know that I see this courage. I honor it. I recognize the strength it takes to remain gentle in a world that has tried to harden you at every turn.

And I want to create space for this gentleness to flourish not just in private moments, not just in safe relationships, but as an acknowledged, celebrated aspect of who you are. I want to witness your tenderness without ever mistaking it for weakness. I want to receive your softness as the gift it truly is.

Because a world that recognizes the power in Black men's gentleness is a world that is finally ready to see Black men in their full humanity. Not as threats to be feared or stereotypes to be managed, but as complete human beings capable of the full spectrum of emotion, expression, and connection.

That world isn't fully here yet. But you are helping to create it, Beloved. Every time you dare to be gentle in a culture that expects hardness. Every time you choose tenderness in a society that rewards toughness. Every time you remain soft in a world that has given you every reason to become hard.

This is not just personal, it's political. It's not just individual, it's collective. Your gentleness is not just a quality, it's a form of resistance against every system, every message, every experience that has tried to rob you of your full humanity. So I honor the courage in your gentleness, Beloved. I celebrate the strength in your tenderness. I witness the power in your softness.

And I promise to create space where this essential part of you can breathe, can expand, can be recognized not as contradiction to your strength, but as its most profound expression.

With reverence for your revolutionary tenderness.

Always, Me

Chapter 17

Between Faith and Doubt

Dear Beloved,

Faith has always been a complicated inheritance for us.

I've watched you navigate this terrain, the space between what you were taught to believe and what your lived experience has shown you. The distance between the certainties of childhood faith and the questions that have emerged as you've walked your own path.

This journey between faith and doubt is rarely spoken about openly in our communities. We talk about having faith. We celebrate conviction. We honor devotion. But the questions, the wrestling, the moments of uncertainty these often remain private struggles, carried in silence.

But I see your journey, Beloved. The way you still bow your head out of respect when grace is said, even as you wonder about the God being addressed. The way you find peace in certain rituals while questioning the institutions that house them. The way you've held onto the essence of what you were taught while releasing interpretations that no longer serve your spirit.

This is not faithlessness. This is faith evolving. This is spirituality maturing. This is the sacred act of seeking truth with your whole heart, even when that seeking leads through valleys of uncertainty.

I know the weight of religious expectations in our community. How faith has been both shelter and sword protecting us through unimaginable hardship while sometimes being wielded to enforce conformity, to silence questions, to maintain hierarchies that serve some while diminishing others.

I know how the Black church has been both haven and heartbreak a place of profound belonging and spiritual nourishment, and also sometimes a space where parts of yourself had to be hidden, where certain questions couldn't be asked, where doubt was treated as weakness rather than as an essential part of any authentic spiritual journey.

I know the particular burden placed on Black men in religious spaces to be both strong in faith and unquestioning in obedience. To be spiritual leaders without the space to acknowledge spiritual struggles. To embody certainty even in moments of profound questioning.

But Beloved, your doubts do not diminish your depth. Your questions do not reveal a lack of character. Your wrestling does not indicate weakness of spirit.

On the contrary, they reveal the seriousness with which you approach matters of the soul. The integrity with which you seek truth. The courage with which you refuse to settle for inherited answers that don't address your lived questions.

The most profound spiritual journeys have always included seasons of questioning. Periods of wrestling. Moments of doubt that eventually give way to deeper, more authentic faith. Not faith that has never been tested, but faith that has walked through the fire of questioning and emerged more resilient, more nuanced, more genuine.

The religion of their oppressors became a liberating force for our ancestors. How they heard messages of submission but found themes of deliverance. How they took a faith that was used to justify their bondage and reshaped it into a source of resistance, resilience, and hope.

That wasn't blind acceptance. That was spiritual discernment of the highest order the ability to separate life giving truth from death dealing distortion. The wisdom to extract liberation from a tradition that was being used to legitimize oppression. The courage to claim a relationship with the divine that transcended the limited, self-serving interpretations being offered.

That legacy of spiritual discernment lives in you, Beloved. That capacity to question not out of cynicism, but out of a deep hunger for truth. That ability to honor tradition while not being imprisoned by it. That courage to seek a faith that liberates rather than constricts, that expands rather than diminishes, that includes rather than excludes.

Your spiritual journey may not look like what was modeled for you. It may include practices from multiple traditions. It may happen outside the walls of formal religious institutions. It may be more about questions than answers, more about seeking than certainty, more about direct experience than doctrinal adherence.

And that's okay. That's more than okay, it's necessary. Because spirituality that hasn't been questioned, hasn't been tested against lived experience, hasn't been allowed to evolve with deepening understanding, isn't truly yours. It's borrowed. Inherited. Secondhand.

But a faith that has walked through the valley of doubt? A spirituality that has been tested in the fires of lived experience? A relationship with the divine that has survived your hardest questions? That belongs to you in a way that unexamined belief never could.

I know this journey isn't easy. I know the particular challenges of navigating spiritual questions as a Black man in a society that has often used religion to control rather than liberate, to silence rather than empower, to divide rather than unite.

I know the tension of honoring the faith traditions that sustained our people through unimaginable hardship while also acknowledging the ways those same traditions have sometimes perpetuated harmful patterns patriarchy, anti-intellectualism, prosperity gospel materialism that don't serve our collective liberation.

I know the loneliness that can come with asking questions that others aren't asking or aren't comfortable hearing. The isolation that can accompany a spiritual journey that doesn't fit neatly into established categories or communities. The fear that in questioning certain aspects of faith, you might lose access to the very spiritual resources and communal connections that have sustained you.

But Beloved, you are not alone in this journey between faith and doubt. You are part of a long, noble lineage of spiritual seekers who have refused to settle for easy answers or unexamined beliefs. Who have had the courage to ask hard questions, even when those questions led through wilderness seasons. Who have been willing to deconstruct inherited faith in order to reconstruct something more authentic, more aligned with their deepest values, more capable of sustaining them through life's complexities.

This journey is not a departure from faith it's an evolution of it. Not a rejection of spirituality, but a deepening of it. Not an abandonment of the divine, but a more direct, more personal, more authentic relationship with whatever name you give to that which is greater than yourself.

And whatever path your spiritual journey takes, know this: your seeking matters. Your questions are valid. Your doubts don't diminish you, they reveal your integrity, your seriousness, your unwillingness to settle for anything less than truth.

Whether you find yourself in a traditional religious community or creating spiritual practice on your own terms. Whether you use the language of your childhood faith or have found new words to express your relationship with the sacred. Whether you've found answers that satisfy or are still living in the questions. Your spiritual journey is worthy of honor, of space, of respect.

Because ultimately, faith isn't about certainty. It's about trust in the midst of uncertainty. It's not about having all the answers, but about being willing to live the questions. It's not about never doubting, but about continuing to seek even when the path isn't clear.

And that kind of faith tested, questioned, refined, authentic is far more powerful than blind acceptance could ever be. It's the kind of faith that can truly sustain you through life's darkest valleys and highest peaks. The kind that grows with you rather than constraining you. The kind that liberates rather than limits.

So, continue your journey, Beloved. Ask your questions. Honor your doubts. Seek your truth. Create spiritual practice that nourishes rather than depletes you. Find community that makes space for your whole self, including your uncertainties.

And know that in this space between faith and doubt, between what was handed to you and what you're discovering for yourself, something sacred is happening. Something authentic is emerging. Something that belongs uniquely to you, while connecting you to all who have walked this path of seeking before you.

With reverence for your spiritual journey in all its complexity.

Always, Me

Chapter 18

The Legacy You're Already Building

Dear Beloved,

When you think of legacy, what comes to mind?

Is it something tangible property passed down, wealth accumulated, material possessions that outlast a lifetime? Is it something visible achievements recognized, accolades earned, milestones marked by certificates and plaques? Is it something measurable the size of a home, the balance of an account, the number of descendants who carry your name?

These are the legacies our society tends to celebrate, especially for Black men. The visible victories. The material manifestations. The measurable markers of success.

But Beloved, I want to speak of a different kind of legacy. The one you're building in moments so ordinary you might not even recognize their significance. The one that lives not just in what you leave behind, but in how you move through each day. The one that's measured not in possessions or achievements, but in presence, in principle, in the quiet power of consistent love.

This legacy isn't waiting for someday. It isn't dependent on reaching some distant milestone or acquiring some specific status. It's being built right now, in ways both subtle and profound.

It lives in the integrity with which you move through the world how you honor your word, how you treat those who can offer you nothing in return, how you stand by your principles even when it costs you something.

It lives in the dignity with which you face challenges how you maintain your humanity even when others try to strip it from you, how you refuse to be reduced to stereotypes or statistics, how you insist on your full personhood in a world that often tries to flatten Black men into caricatures.

It lives in the tenderness you show to those who need it how you speak to children at eye level, how you offer comfort without minimizing pain, how you create safety through your presence rather than fear through your power.

It lives in the boundaries you maintain, how you say no to what diminishes you, how you protect your peace, how you model self-respect by refusing to accept disrespect.

It lives in the vulnerability you dare to show how you admit when you're wrong, how you ask for help when you need it, how you express emotion even when you were taught that emotion makes you weak.

These aren't small things, Beloved. These are the threads from which the fabric of legacy is woven. These are the seeds from which forests of influence grow. These are the moments that shape not just your life, but the lives of everyone you touch.

I think about how legacy works in our community how it's not always about grand gestures or public recognition. How some of our most important cultural inheritances were passed down not through formal institutions, but through daily practices. How wisdom was transmitted not in lecture halls, but at kitchen tables. How values were instilled not through proclamations, but through consistent example.

Your grandfather may not have left you property, but he left you the example of a man who showed up every day, who did what needed to be done without complaint, who treated others with a dignity that transcended his circumstances. Your uncle may not have left you money, but he left you the memory of how he listened when you spoke, how he believed in you when you didn't believe in yourself, how he made space for your dreams in a world that often tried to limit them.

These legacies may not be recognized by society at large. They may not be celebrated in history books or commemorated with monuments. But they are no less powerful for their quietness. No less significant for their subtlety. No less valuable for being measured in moments rather than monuments.

And you, Beloved, are continuing this lineage of quiet impact. Building legacy not just through what you achieve or acquire, but through how you live. Through the consistency of your character. Through the quality of your presence. Through the courage of your convictions.

Every time you choose integrity over expediency, you're building a legacy.

Every time you offer dignity to someone society has deemed unworthy, you're building a legacy.

Every time you show up fully, not just physically, but emotionally, mentally, spiritually, you're building a legacy.

Every time you break a cycle of harm rather than perpetuating it, you're building a legacy.

These choices may seem small in the moment. They may go unrecognized, uncelebrated, unrewarded by a world that often values flash over substance, appearance over reality, immediate gain over long term impact.

But their effects ripple outward in ways you may never fully see. The child who witnesses your integrity learns what it means to live by principle rather than convenience. The friend who experiences your consistent presence learns what true reliability looks like. The partner who receives your vulnerability learns that strength includes softness, not just stoicism.

And these lessons embodied, experienced, absorbed through relationship rather than instruction become part of who they are. Part of how they move through the world. Part of what they, in turn, pass on to others.

That's how legacy works at its most profound level. Not through what we leave behind when we're gone, but through how we influence others while we're here. Not through grand gestures or public achievements, but through the accumulated impact of daily choices. Not through what we say about our values, but through how we live them.

I know the pressure Black men face to build certain kinds of legacies. The expectation to provide materially, to achieve visibly, to succeed according to standards that weren't created with you in mind and often actively work against you. I know the weight of feeling that your worth is measured by what you can show for your life rather than by who you are in it.

But Beloved, I want you to know: The legacy you're already building through how you live each day is profound. The impact you're having through your presence, your principles, your consistent love is immeasurable. The difference you're making through choices that may seem small but carry the weight of your character is significant beyond calculation.

You don't have to wait until you've reached some arbitrary marker of success to believe that your life matters, that your influence counts, that your legacy is being built. You don't have to achieve some specific status or acquire some particular possession to know that you're making a difference that will outlast your lifetime.

The truth is, legacy isn't primarily about what you leave behind when you're gone. It's about what you're giving while you're here. It's not measured in possessions or achievements, but in presence, in principle, in the quiet power of consistent love.

And by that measure, Beloved, your legacy is already rich beyond measure. Already significant beyond calculation. Already worthy of celebration and recognition.

So, continue building this legacy of integrity, dignity, tenderness, boundaries, of vulnerability. Continue showing up fully, loving deeply, standing firmly for what matters most. Continue breaking cycles that need to be broken and creating new patterns that heal rather than harm.

Know that these choices matter. That their impact extends far beyond what you can see in the moment. That they are creating ripples that will continue long after the stone has sunk beneath the surface.

And know that I see this legacy you're building. I honor it. I celebrate it. Not just for what it will mean someday, but for what it means right now a life lived with intention, with integrity, with the courage to be fully human in a world that has often denied Black men their full humanity.

That, Beloved, is a legacy worthy of your name. Worthy of your ancestors. Worthy of all who will come after you, carrying forward the impact of a life well lived not just in grand moments, but in the sacred ordinary of each day.

With profound respect for the legacy you're already building.

Always, Me

Chapter 19

When Laughter Becomes Your Shield and Your Medicine

Dear Beloved,

There's a particular kind of laughter I've heard from you, one that rises from somewhere deep and ancient. A laughter that doesn't just express joy but transforms pain. A laughter that doesn't merely entertain but sustains.

It's the laughter that erupts in barbershops when stories get passed around like communion. It's the chuckle that punctuates difficult truths to make them easier to swallow. It's the full-bodied roar that sometimes comes after recounting something that should have broken you, but somehow didn't.

This laughter Black joy in its purest form is both your shield and your medicine.

I've watched how you use it as protection. How humor becomes armor in hostile environments. How a well-timed joke can deflect tension, disarm aggression, create breathing room in spaces where your very presence is treated as a threat. How laughter can be a way of saying, "You can't touch the core of me. You can't reach the place where my joy lives."

This strategic use of humor isn't new. Our ancestors wielded it masterfully, finding ways to laugh even in the shadow of the unspeakable. Using coded jokes to communicate truths that would have been dangerous to express directly. Creating moments of levity that preserved their humanity in systems designed to strip it away.

That legacy of protective laughter lives in you. That ability to find humor even in hardship. That gift for using wit as a weapon against dehumanization. That talent for transforming potential humiliation into self-determined hilarity.

But your laughter isn't just a shield, Beloved. It's also medicine.

I've seen how it heals you from the inside out. How it releases tension that would otherwise settle in your body as pain. How it creates connection in moments of isolation. How it restores perspective when problems start to seem insurmountable. How it returns you to yourself when the world has tried to make you a stranger in your own skin.

There's science behind this medicine how laughter reduces stress hormones, boosts immune function, triggers the release of endorphins, and creates neural pathways associated with resilience. But long before researchers documented these effects, our people knew intuitively that joy was not a luxury but a necessity. That laughter wasn't frivolous but fundamental to survival.

I think about the blues tradition, how it transformed suffering into art, pain into poetry, and struggle into song. How it didn't deny the reality of hardship but refused to be defined by it. How it made space for both the wound and the healing, both the truth of pain and the possibility of joy.

Your laughter carries the same wisdom. It doesn't pretend that life hasn't been hard or that injustice doesn't exist. It doesn't gloss over difficulty or deny reality. Instead, it insists that hardship isn't the whole story. That pain doesn't get the final word. That joy remains possible even in the most challenging circumstances.

This is revolutionary, Beloved. In a world that has often expected Black men to be either threatening or entertaining, your authentic laughter the kind that comes from your core, not from performing for others' comfort is an act of radical self-possession. It declares that your joy belongs to you, not to those who would use it or constrain it or misinterpret it.

In a society that has often denied Black men the full range of human emotion, your laughter asserts your right to feel deeply, to express freely, to experience the entire spectrum of human experience including joy, including humor, including the healing power of not taking everything (including yourself) too seriously.

In a culture that has often treated Black pain as either invisible or spectacle, your ability to transform that pain through humor is a form of alchemical magic. It doesn't erase the hurt, but it prevents the hurt from having the last laugh. It doesn't deny the struggle, but it refuses to let struggle become your only story.

I know there are times when laughter feels impossible. When the weight is too heavy, the injustice too raw, the pain too fresh. I know there are spaces where your joy is misinterpreted, your humor misunderstood, your laughter treated with suspicion rather than recognized as the life affirming force it truly is.

I know the particular burden Black men carry to modulate your expression in public spaces, to calculate how your joy might be perceived, to consider whether your laughter will be read as aggression or disrespect rather than the natural expression of a fully human being experiencing a moment of delight.

And still, you laugh. Still, you find moments of joy. Still, you refuse to let pain be the only story you live or tell.

That's not just resilience, Beloved. That's resistance.

Because joy has always been an act of defiance for Black folks. A declaration that despite everything designed to crush our spirit, to dampen our light, to silence our laughter, we still find reasons to celebrate. We still create beauty. We still insist on experiencing the full range of human emotion, including the sweet relief of humor, the healing balm of joy.

Your laughter carries this legacy forward. It honors those who found ways to laugh even when freedom was just a dream. It channels the wisdom of those who understood that survival required not just endurance, but joy. It continues the tradition of those who used humor not just to cope, but to create community, to preserve dignity, to imagine possibilities beyond present circumstances.

So, laugh, Beloved. Let that deep, soul stirring laughter rise from your belly and echo in the air around you. Let it serve as both protection and healing, both shield and medicine. Let it create space for others to access their own joy, to remember their own capacity for delight, to reconnect with their own humanity.

Let your laughter be authentic rather than performative. Let it come from a place of self-determination rather than expectation. Let it express the fullness of who you are rather than conforming to what others think Black joy should look or sound like.

And know that in those moments of genuine laughter, whether it's a quiet chuckle or a room filling roar, you are practicing a form of freedom. You are continuing a tradition of finding light even in darkness. You are engaging in a revolutionary act of self-care and communal healing.

Your joy matters, Beloved. Not just as relief from struggle, but as an essential aspect of a fully lived life. Not just as momentary escape, but as sustaining force. Not just as personal pleasure, but as political statement.

In a world that has often tried to limit Black men to expressions of anger or stoicism, your laughter declares that you contain multitudes. That you can hold both rage at injustice and capacity for joy. That you can acknowledge pain without being defined by it. That you can transform suffering without denying its reality.

This is the medicine our community has always created for itself, the ability to alchemize pain into art, struggle into strength, and hardship into humor. The wisdom of knowing that joy isn't what comes after liberation; it's what sustains us on the journey toward it.

So let your laughter ring out, Beloved. Let it serve as both protection and healing. Let it shield you from those who would diminish your humanity and heal the places where life has left its scars. Let it connect you to a lineage of Black joy that stretches back generations and forward into a future where our descendants will still be finding reasons to throw their heads back and roar with life affirming delight.

Your laughter is not just an expression, it's inheritance. Not just pleasure, it's power. Not just momentary relief, it's revolutionary resistance against everything that would rob you of your right to the full spectrum of human emotion.

And in its medicine, may you find not just healing for yourself, but connection to all who have used joy as resistance, humor as survival, laughter as the ultimate declaration that life, with all its hardships, remains stubbornly, gloriously worth living.

With reverence for the revolutionary power of your joy.

Always, Me

Chapter 20

The Brotherhood You Need

Dear Beloved,

There's a particular kind of loneliness that comes with being a Black man in this world one that exists even when you're surrounded by people. Even when you're "successful." Even when, by all outward appearances, you're connected.

It's the loneliness of holding things you don't feel safe to share. Of carrying questions, you don't feel permitted to ask. Of experiencing pain, you've been taught to swallow rather than speak. Of navigating a world that often sees your strength but misses your humanity.

And in that loneliness, there is a particular kind of hunger for brotherhood. Not just for company or networking or surface level connection, but for the deep, soul nourishing bond that comes from being truly seen, truly heard, truly known by other men who understand your journey because they're walking their own version of it.

I've watched you navigate male friendships over the years. The easy camaraderie around sports and music. The shared jokes and ritual greetings. The surface level check ins that rarely venture beneath "I'm good, man" even when you're anything but good.

These connections matter. They provide community, continuity, and a sense of belonging. But I also see the hunger for something deeper. Something that goes beyond shared activities to shared vulnerability. Beyond common interests to mutual understanding. Beyond "what's up" to "what's really going on with you."

This hunger isn't weakness, Beloved. It's wisdom. The recognition that no man is meant to walk alone. That even the strongest among us need spaces where we can lay down the weight for a while. That true resilience comes not from never needing support, but from knowing how to receive it when it's offered and how to ask for it when it's not.

Our ancestors understood this. They created circles of brotherhood that sustained them through unimaginable hardship. Spaces where they could speak truths that weren't safe to voice elsewhere. Where they could share burdens that were too heavy to carry alone. Where they could receive the kind of witnessing that reminded them of their humanity in a world determined to deny it.

These weren't just social gatherings. They were survival mechanisms. Sacred spaces of mutual recognition and support that made it possible to endure, to resist, to maintain dignity and purpose in the face of systems designed to strip these away.

That legacy of brotherhood lives in your bones, Beloved. That hunger for meaningful connection with other men isn't foreign to who you are it's intrinsic to it. Part of your inheritance. Part of what makes you human.

But I also know the barriers that exist to this kind of connection. The messages you've received about what male friendship should look like. The cultural scripts that limit intimacy between men, especially Black men. The fear that vulnerability will be mistaken for weakness, that emotional honesty will be met with rejection, that reaching for deeper connection will be misinterpreted or weaponized.

I know how these barriers have shaped your approach to friendship. How they've created hesitation where there might have been openness. How they've encouraged you to keep conversations at the level of sports statistics and career achievements rather than venturing into the territory of dreams and doubts, fears and failures, questions and quests.

But Beloved, what if those deeper connections aren't just possible, but essential? What if the brotherhood you hunger for isn't a luxury, but a necessity for your well-being, your growth, your ability to thrive rather than merely survive?

What if the vulnerability you've been taught to avoid is actually the doorway to the very connection you seek?

I think about the research showing how isolation impacts men's health physical, mental, emotional, spiritual. How lack of meaningful connection is linked to everything from heart disease to depression, from substance abuse to suicide. How the stoicism that's often celebrated as strength can become a prison that separates men from the very support they need to truly be strong.

This isn't just personal; it's systemic. A culture that teaches men, especially Black men, that needing others is weakness. That emotional self-sufficiency is the marker of manhood. That vulnerability is dangerous rather than courageous.

But what if the opposite is true? What if true strength lies not in isolation but in connection? Not in self-sufficiency but in mutual support? Not in emotional invulnerability but in the courage to be seen in your full humanity?

I believe it does, Beloved. I believe the brotherhood you hunger for is not just possible but waiting to be created through the very vulnerability you've been taught to avoid.

It might not look like the friendships you see portrayed in the media. It might not revolve around traditional markers of male bonding. It might require creating new scripts, new rituals, new ways of being together that make space for both strength and tenderness, both achievement and struggle, both laughter and tears.

It might mean being the one who goes first, who asks the deeper question, who shares the honest struggle, who creates space for conversation that goes beyond the surface. It might mean risking rejection or misunderstanding in the pursuit of connection that truly nourishes.

But Beloved, that risk is worth taking. Because the alternative continuing to hunger for brotherhood while settling for its pale imitation exacts its own cost. A cost paid in the solation masquerades as independence. In loneliness disguised as self-sufficiency. In the slow erosion of well-being that comes from carrying burdens that were meant to be shared.

I've seen glimpses of what's possible when Black men create spaces of authentic brotherhood. The healing that happens when pain is spoken rather than swallowed. The wisdom that emerges when questions are voiced rather than suppressed. The strength that's found, not in pretending to have all the answers, but in the courage to say, "I don't know" or "I'm struggling" or "I need help."

These spaces exist, Beloved. Sometimes in formal settings like men's groups or therapeutic communities. Sometimes in informal gatherings of friends who've made a commitment to go deeper. Sometimes in one on one relationships that have evolved beyond surface connection to soul level witnessing.

And if you can't find these spaces, you can create them. Not by waiting for others to go first, but by being the one who opens the door to deeper conversation. Not by expecting perfection, but by being willing to start small and build slowly. Not by demanding vulnerability from others, but by offering your own as an invitation rather than a requirement.

This isn't about performative emotion or forced disclosure. It's about creating spaces where authenticity is welcomed rather than judged. Where strength includes the courage to acknowledge struggle. Where brotherhood means not just showing up for the celebrations but walking together through the valleys.

You deserve this kind of brotherhood, Beloved. Not because you're weak, but because you're human. Not because you can't handle life on your own, but because you were never meant to. Not because you need fixing, but because you need witnessing the kind that reminds you of your inherent worth, your fundamental belonging, your unquestionable humanity.

And other men in your life deserve this too. They hunger for it just as you do, even if they've never named that hunger. They long for spaces where they can lay down the mask, even if they've never admitted that longing. They need the very witnessing that you yourself need, even if they've been taught to deny that need.

So, reach for this brotherhood, Beloved. Not as something extra or optional, but as essential nourishment for your spirit. Not as a sign of weakness, but as an expression of wisdom. Not as a departure from strength, but as its deepest embodiment.

Because true brotherhood isn't just about having people to do things with. It's about having people to be with. People who see beyond your achievements to your essence. People who hear beyond your words to your heart. People who know beyond your public self to your private truth.

That kind of brotherhood doesn't just enhance life; it sustains it. It doesn't just add connection; it restores wholeness. It doesn't just provide company it offers communion of the kind that reminds you who you are when the world has tried to make you forget.

You need this brotherhood, Beloved. And somewhere, other men are waiting for exactly the kind of witnessing that you yourself can offer. The kind that says, "I see you not just your strength, but your struggle. Not just your achievements, but your doubts. Not just your public self, but your whole humanity."

That's the brotherhood you hunger for. That's the brotherhood you deserve. That's the brotherhood that waits to be created through the very vulnerability you've been taught to avoid.

With belief in the healing power of true brotherhood.

Always, Me

Chapter 21

Reclaiming Your Narrative

Dear Beloved,

From the moment you entered this world, stories have been written about you.

Stories about what it means to be Black. Stories about what it means to be a man. Stories about what happens when these two identities intersect in a body that breathes and dreams and loves and fears.

Some of these stories were whispered as warnings by those who loved you trying to prepare you for a world that might not see your humanity before it sees your skin. Some were shouted as judgments by those who feared you projecting their own darkness onto your light. Some were woven into the very fabric of the society you move through embedded in policies, portrayed in media, perpetuated in everyday interactions.

These stories have power. They shape how others see you. How institutions treat you. How opportunities open or close before you even reach for the door.

But their greatest power lies in how they can seep into your own understanding of yourself. How they can become the lens through which you view your own possibilities. How they can transform from external narratives to internal beliefs so seamless you might mistake them for your own voice.

"Black men are dangerous."

"Black men are athletes, not intellectuals."

"Black men are absent fathers."

"Black men are hypersexual."

"Black men are angry."

"Black men are..."

The list goes on. Narrow stories. Flat characterizations. Stereotypes masquerading as truth.

But Beloved, I want to speak a different truth today:

These stories were never yours. They were never about you. They were never even about truth.

They were about control. About justifying systems of oppression. About making inequality seem natural rather than constructed. About limiting the fullness of who you could become by telling you who you were allowed to be.

And the most revolutionary act you can undertake is to reclaim your narrative. To take back the pen. To write your own story not in reaction to the false ones, but in alignment with your deepest truth.

This isn't simple work. It requires recognizing the stories that have been written onto your life without your consent. Identifying the narratives that have shaped your sense of possibility, your understanding of your own worth, your vision of what you deserve.

It requires asking: Where did I learn this belief about myself? Who benefits from me believing this? What evidence in my actual lived experience contradicts this story?

It requires the courage to question even the stories that seem protective. The ones that taught you to be small; to be safe. To be silent to survive. To expect less to avoid disappointment. To armor up to prevent harm.

These stories may have served a purpose once. They may have been passed down with love by those trying to help you navigate a hostile world. They may have protected you in certain contexts, at certain times.

But protection that limits your full expression isn't truly protection at all. Safety purchased at the cost of your authenticity isn't truly safety. Survival that requires you to abandon parts of yourself isn't truly living.

You deserve more than survival, Beloved. You deserve to thrive. To expand. To explore the full range of who you are and who you might become, unconstrained by narratives that were never designed to honor your complexity or celebrate your potential.

Our ancestors resisted the dehumanizing stories written about them. I recall how they created counter narratives through art, through music, through literature, through everyday acts of dignity and self-definition; how they insisted on their humanity in a world determined to deny it.

That resistance lives in you. That capacity to define yourself beyond the limiting stories. That power to create new narratives that reflect your truth rather than someone else's agenda.

I've seen glimpses of it in the moments when you refuse to be reduced to a stereotype. When you express complexity that defies easy categorization. When you show up with a fullness that challenges others' narrow expectations. When you insist, through your very being, that you are more than the stories that have been written about you.

These aren't small acts, Beloved. They are revolutionary. Each time you express an emotion that doesn't fit the "angry Black man" narrative, you are rewriting the story. Each time you demonstrate intellectual depth that defies the "athlete not scholar" stereotype, you are reclaiming the narrative. Each time you show tenderness that contradicts the "dangerous Black male" myth, you are taking back the pen.

But reclaiming your narrative isn't just about proving stereotypes wrong. It's not about living in reaction to false stories. It's about the freedom to live from your center, guided by your own values, your own vision, your own understanding of who you are and what matters most.

It's about recognizing that you are not a character in someone else's story. You are the author of your own life. The protagonist of your own journey. The creator of meaning in your own experience.

This doesn't mean denying the reality of systemic racism or the impact of historical trauma. It doesn't mean pretending that external barriers don't exist or that structural inequalities don't shape opportunity. It doesn't mean adopting a naive "just think positive" approach to very real challenges.

It means refusing to let those external realities define your internal sense of who you are and what's possible. It means distinguishing between the conditions you're navigating and the essence of who you are. It means recognizing that while you didn't create the systems you're moving through, you have agency in how you respond to them, how you make meaning from your experiences, how you define yourself within and beyond the constraints you encounter.

Reclaiming your narrative means getting curious about the stories you've internalized. The beliefs about yourself that feel so natural you don't even recognize them as acquired rather than inherent. The limitations you've accepted as truth rather than questioning as constructed.

It means asking:

Who would I be if I hadn't been told who I should be?

What would I want if I hadn't been taught what I should want?

How would I express myself if I hadn't learned what expressions were acceptable?

These are not abstract philosophical questions, Beloved. They are pathways to liberation. Because the stories we believe about ourselves shape the lives we create, the relationships we form, the dreams we pursue, the healing we seek, the joy we allow ourselves to experience.

When you believe the narrative that Black men must be strong at all costs, you deny yourself the healing that comes through vulnerability.

When you accept the story that Black men must be providers before all else, you limit your ability to explore purpose beyond productivity.

When you internalize the narrative that Black men's worth is measured by material success, you miss the richness of contribution that comes through presence, through wisdom, through the quality of your character rather than the quantity of your possessions.

Reclaiming your narrative means questioning these stories not to reject all guidance from those who came before you, but to discern which inherited wisdom truly serves your becoming and which inherited limitations can be gently laid down.

It means recognizing that tradition can be both anchor and barrier honoring what sustains while releasing what constrains. It means understanding that respect for elders and ancestors can coexist with charting your own course, defining your own values, and creating your own meaning.

This is sacred work, Beloved. Work that requires courage, discernment, compassion for yourself as you unlearn limiting stories and create new ones more aligned with your truth. Work that happens not all at once, but in small moments of choice, of awareness, of intentional self-definition.

And you don't have to do this work alone. Find others who are engaged in their own narrative reclamation. Create spaces where you can speak your emerging truth and have it witnessed without judgment. Seek out stories in books, in film, in conversation that reflect the complexity and possibility you know exists beyond the narrow narratives.

Because when you reclaim your narrative, you don't just liberate yourself. You create possibility for others still trapped in limiting stories. You expand what's imaginable for those coming after you. You contribute to a world where Black men are seen not as flat stereotypes but as full human beings complex, contradictory, constantly evolving.

Your story matters, Beloved. Not the one that was written about you, but the one you are writing with your choices, your voice, your presence, your particular way of moving through the world.

Tell it boldly. Tell it truly. Tell it in a way that honors both where you've come from and where you're going. Tell it not to prove anything to anyone, but to claim the freedom that comes from defining yourself rather than being defined.

Because when you reclaim your narrative, you reclaim your power. Not power over others, but power from within. The power to create meaning. The power to define value. The power to determine what success looks like, what love looks like, what a life well lived looks like on your own terms.

That's not just personal liberation, Beloved. That's revolutionary resistance against every system, every message, every experience that has tried to tell you who you are instead of creating space for you to discover and declare it for yourself.

Your narrative belongs to you. Reclaim it. Rewrite it. Live it. Share it. And watch how the world rearranges itself to accommodate the truth of who you really are.

With belief in your power to author your own story.

Always, Me

Chapter 22

The Future Your Ancestors Dreamed

Dear Beloved,

There is a thread that connects you to those who came before a golden thread of hope, of resistance, of dreams deferred but never abandoned.

Our ancestors are not distant figures frozen in black and white photographs, but flesh and blood people who loved and struggled and hoped with the same intensity that pulses through your veins today. People who planted seeds they knew they would never live to see bloom. People who dreamed futures they knew their own eyes would never witness.

They dreamed of you, Beloved.

Not you specifically, perhaps. Not your name or your face, or the particular constellation of gifts that makes you uniquely yourself. But they dreamed of the possibility you represent. The freedom you embody. The opportunities you navigate even with their complications and contradictions that were once unimaginable horizons.

They dreamed of a descendant who could walk with his head high. Who could love openly. Who could speak his mind without fear of the lash or the rope. Who could pursue education, create art, build business, raise children, worship freely, vote his conscience, own property, travel widely, rest deeply.

They dreamed of you.

And in moments when the weight of today's struggles feels overwhelming when racism still shows its face in new masks, when justice still seems more promise than practice, when equality still feels more theoretical than lived, I want you to remember this truth:

You are the future our ancestors dreamed of.

Not the end point of their dreaming, but the continuation. Not the fulfillment of all they hoped for, but the living proof that their hopes were not in vain. Not the completion of the journey, but evidence that the arc they helped bend is indeed curving, however slowly, toward justice.

This isn't about placing the burden of their unfulfilled dreams on your shoulders. It's not about demanding perfection or achievement or some narrow definition of "making them proud." It's not about using their sacrifice to shame you into being someone you're not or doing something that doesn't align with your own purpose.

It's about recognizing the profound connection between their dreaming and your breathing. Between their resistance and your existence. Between what they dared to imagine and what you get to embody.

I think about the specific dreams they might have held. The grandfather who couldn't vote dreaming of a grandson who could not just cast a ballot, but perhaps run for office. The great grandmother who cleaned other people's homes dreaming of a great granddaughter who could own property, build wealth, create a sanctuary of her own. The ancestor who had to hide his reading dreaming of descendants who could not just learn freely, but teach, write, publish, speak truth to power without hiding their literacy or their brilliance.

These weren't just dreams of material success or individual achievement. They were dreams of dignity. Of self-determination. Of the freedom to be fully human in a world that tried to deny Black humanity. Of the right to pursue purpose, to experience joy, to love and be loved without the crushing weight of systemic oppression determining every outcome.

And while we haven't reached the fullness of what they dreamed while injustice still persists, while new forms of oppression have emerged alongside the old, your life represents progress they fought for. Freedom they marched for. Possibilities they prayed for.

You are the future they dreamed. And now you get to dream the future that those who come after you will embody.

What will that future look like, Beloved? What seeds are you planting that you may never see bloom? What dreams are you nurturing that may only find fulfillment in generations yet unborn?

These aren't just philosophical questions. They're invitations to see your life as part of something larger than yourself. To recognize that the choices you make today how you love, how you resist, how you create, how you heal, are shaping possibilities for those who will come after you, just as your ancestors' choices shaped possibilities for you.

This perspective doesn't diminish the very real challenges you face. It doesn't sugarcoat the work still to be done. It doesn't pretend that historical progress has been steady or sufficient. It doesn't ignore the ways that old oppressions have shape shifted into new forms, the ways that freedom gained in one arena has been countered by constraints imposed in another.

But it does offer a longer view. A reminder that you stand in a lineage of dreamers and doers who refused to let the conditions of their present determine the horizons of their imagination.

142

Who insisted on envisioning freedom they might never personally experience. Who understood that revolution isn't just about tearing down what doesn't work, it's about creating and nurturing what does.

Your ancestors didn't just resist oppression. They cultivated joy. They created beauty. They built community. They preserved traditions. They innovated new forms of expression. They loved fiercely. They celebrated abundantly. They found ways to thrive even in soil that was never meant to support their flourishing.

That legacy of creativity, of resilience, of visionary imagination lives in you, Beloved. It's not separate from the legacy of struggle and resistance it's intertwined with it. The ability to dream beyond current constraints. To create what hasn't existed before. To insist on joy as a form of resistance. To love as a revolutionary act.

I think about how your ancestors held these tensions fighting against what was while creating what could be. How they balanced clear eyed recognition of present injustice with unshakable faith in future possibility. How they found ways to celebrate even while continuing to struggle, to create beauty even in the midst of ugliness, to nurture community even when forces worked to tear it apart.

This too is your inheritance. This capacity to hold the both/and. To acknowledge how far we still have to go while honoring how far we've come. To work for change while finding joy in the journey. To dream of futures you may never see while creating as much of that future as possible in your present.

What dreams are you nurturing, Beloved? What seeds are you planting? What future are you imagining that might seem impossible in this moment but could become reality for those who come after you?

Maybe it's a world where Black men are seen in their full humanity not as threats or stereotypes, but as complex individuals with the full range of human emotions, aspirations, and needs.

Maybe it's a society where economic justice is reality, not rhetoric where the racial wealth gap has been closed, where access to opportunity isn't determined by zip code, where everyone has what they need to not just survive but thrive.

Maybe it's a future where the environment has been healed where the communities that have borne the brunt of environmental racism now have clean air, clean water, access to nature, and leadership roles in creating sustainable solutions.

Maybe it's a time when our political systems truly represent all people where voting rights are protected and expanded, where gerrymandering and voter suppression are relics of the past, where elected officials actually reflect the diversity of the communities they serve.

Or maybe your dreams are more intimate. A future where Black families have the resources and support to heal generational trauma. Where Black children grow up knowing their history, their worth, their limitless potential. Where Black love is celebrated rather than pathologized. Where Black joy is recognized as resistance, as birthright, as essential rather than frivolous.

Whatever future you're dreaming, know that the very act of dreaming it matters. Your vision creates possibility. Your imagination helps bend the arc. Your refusal to accept current limitations as permanent boundaries helps create openings for those who will come after you.

This isn't about placing the entire burden of social change on your shoulders. It's not about suggesting that individual dreams can overcome systemic barriers without collective action, policy change, and structural transformation. It's not about magical thinking that ignores the very real work required to create more just futures.

It's about recognizing that dreaming is part of that work. That imagination is a necessary precursor to creation. That the ability to envision what doesn't yet exist is the first step toward bringing it into being.

Your ancestors understood this. They dreamed you, Beloved. They dreamed possibilities they would never live to see. They dreamed freedoms they would never personally experience. And those dreams combined with action, with sacrifice, with persistent effort helped create openings that allowed you to exist as you do today.

Now you get to continue that sacred work. To dream futures that may seem impossible in this moment. To plant seeds you may never see bloom. To bend the arc a little further toward justice, knowing that the full realization of that justice may come long after your lifetime.

This is not a burden, Beloved. It's a blessing. The blessing of being part of something larger than yourself. Of knowing that your life is connected to those who came before and those who will come after. Of recognizing that while individual lives are finite, collective dreaming and striving creates ripples that extend far beyond any single lifetime.

You are the future your ancestors dreamed. And the dreams you nurture today are creating possibilities for futures yet to come. Futures where those who follow you will look back and say, with gratitude and reverence: They dreamed us. They fought for us. They created openings that allowed us to exist as we do today.

What a sacred legacy to inherit. What a sacred legacy to create.

With reverence for the dreams that brought you here and the dreams you're nurturing for those to come,

Always, Me

Made in the USA
Monee, IL
12 July 2025

20821648R00089